FROM THE BRONX TO BOCA

MIMI'S STORY

THE FIRST 94 YEARS

Mimi Sherman

To order additional copies of this book, contact:
Xlibris
844-714-8691
www.Xlibris.com
Orders@Xlibris.com

ISBN: Softcover   978-1-6698-6804-0
       Hardcover   978-1-6698-6805-7
       EBook   978-1-6698-6803-3

Print information available on the last page

Rev. date: 03/10/2023

PROLOGUE

This book is a compilation of questions and answers about my ninety-four years of loving the life I have lived from the time I was a little girl until now. I have put this together so my children, grandchildren, and great-grandchildren and their descendants will know . . . "who I am."

I have attempted to answer questions about my childhood, my parents, my brother, my children, the people who have affected my life, and all my other relatives. I have answered questions about my career as a teacher and my sweater business. You will learn about my tennis experiences and my creative abilities. And, of course, I will tell you about how I met Harry, whom I love very much. In all, I have no regrets. I have lived life to the fullest, and it is my intention to keep going.

The motivation for my decision to write this book was after a question-and-answer interview I did with my granddaughter Jessi. It was a school project entitled "The American Dream." I might mention that she got an A. I sent copies of her essay to members of my family, and my grandson Alex called me and said I should write a book in my own words telling my life story. And so I decided to write my memoir in the form of questions and answers.

I hope you enjoy reading the book as much as I enjoyed writing it.

DEDICATION

Without the help of Harry, I would not have been able to complete this book.
His help in editing and suggestions made the writing so much easier.

CHAPTER 1

What Was It like Growing Up with Immigrant Parents?

How Did They Impact Your Life since They Did Not Speak English?

Where I lived, everybody was an immigrant, and I lived in the Northeast Bronx in a one-bedroom apartment. I had a younger brother Morty. We had twin beds in the bedroom where he and I slept and a Castro Convertible sofa in the living room where my parents slept. They opened it every night and closed it every morning.

My parents came from Poland in the 1920s. There was a quota system then, and they had to wait two years before they could come here. In addition, they had to be sponsored by someone—usually a family member or friend. They had to have a place to live and had to have a job waiting for them. My mother (Rose) and father (Murray) were sponsored by their older brothers who had arrived in this country several years earlier. In 1927, my parents met at a reunion banquet arranged by immigrants from Lublin, Poland. They were married later that year, and I was born in 1928.

They spoke Yiddish and Polish. They had to learn English, and that was very difficult. As a child, I had to learn to speak their language, so I spoke Yiddish. And when I started school, I finally learned how to speak English. Of course, I spoke broken English at first; and luckily for me, I was able to progress in school very well.

My father became a housepainter because his brother, who had sponsored him, was a housepainter. His brother eventually became the foreman of the job. My father's ambition was to become a foreman as well. It would require him to purchase a car to carry supplies and men to do the next painting job. He was unable to afford a car. This created a lot of stress. Since his work was seasonal, there were many days and weeks when he did not work, which caused hostility between my parents.

My mother worked as a dressmaker in Manhattan. She had to travel every day for an hour there and an hour back to the Bronx by train. When she arrived at her station, she would stop at all the various stores—there were no supermarkets—and bring home bundles for dinner. She was unable to bring home food for the next day as well because we did not have a refrigerator. We had an icebox. A man would bring a large junk of ice to put in this icebox where we kept our food cold. He had to walk up a flight of steps with the ice, carrying it on his back. He delivered ice every few days.

She had to carry these heavy bundles for several blocks until she got to our apartment in a big building, and then she would first have to prepare dinner. When I was twelve years old, she said, "Now you are old enough to prepare dinner every night." That's what I did from twelve on. I had to do it! We always ate together. We exchanged stories of our experiences that day. This bonded our family.

As I started school, my parents realized that they had to learn English, so they decided that we were only to speak English at home. This would help them learn to speak English better. At the same time, they wanted me to learn how to read and write in Yiddish, so they sent me to a Jewish school about six blocks from our apartment and another five blocks from my elementary school. I would go after school from 3:30 p.m. to 5:00 p.m., three days each week. I had to learn the Hebrew alphabet, which was quite difficult. I went through elementary and high school and was the valedictorian at graduation.

My parents decided to go to night school to further their knowledge of the English language. My mother, poor woman, could not handle night school. She was exhausted from working so hard. I tried to tutor her as well, but she was not able to do it. She was never able to read or write. She was able to work with numbers, however. I was very embarrassed that my mother was illiterate.

My father, however, enjoyed night school, went for many years, and finally completed sixth grade. He would read the *New York Times* and the *Forward* each day. He always emphasized how important it is to be educated. Among his friends, a sixth-grade education was comparable to a college degree today.

MIMI SHERMAN

CHAPTER 2

How Was Your School Experience?
How Difficult Was It for You?

My elementary school consisted of six months' semesters. It had 1A and 1B, then 2A and 2B, and so forth. I skipped from 1B to 2B. Everyone made a fuss over me in school. I had no idea what skipping meant, and neither did my mother. We had to ask a neighbor to explain it to us. I found out that I did not have to go to 2A but instead go straight to 2B. I was very happy and proud. I had been practicing skipping-hopping. I skipped again from 5B to 6B. This time, I was aware that I did not have to take 6A. My elementary school, PS 89, went from half-day kindergarten to eighth grade. I was captain of all the monitors in the school, and I carried the flag every Friday morning when we had an assembly program.

I then went on to Christopher Columbus High School. I excelled in math and took four years of it. There were no advanced placement classes or SATs. Very few students went on to college. I didn't know anything about college. One day, my guidance counselor called me to her office. She discussed my applying to college. She said that my grades were good enough to get into one of the city colleges. I applied to City College Uptown in New York. I was accepted and received a full scholarship.

I did not participate in many activities in high school, particularly after school. I spent three afternoons learning Yiddish. On the remaining two days, I joined a math team, a softball team where I was the pitcher, and a radio club where I learned to use special effects on the radio. I really didn't have time nor the inclination for more than that.

When I think of the hardships we experienced as children, I cannot believe that we were able to withstand it all. There was never anyone who could help me with homework, a project, or a test. They did not understand what I was learning. I had to do everything myself. Thankfully, I was able to help my brother. Besides this, we were left alone all day. We had to walk about five blocks to PS 89 in all kinds of weather whether it rained, it poured, or it snowed. I remember coming into school soaking wet, and that is how I had to sit all day, soaking wet. There was no one to call (we did not have a phone), there was no one to help us, and you just had to do it yourself! My parents worked all day, Monday through Friday. You just felt that this was the way of life, and you had to accept it. When we went to high school, it was much worse because the school was ten blocks from our apartment, and the circumstances were the same. Think of what we have today for our children, grandchildren, and great-grandchildren!

My Parents

Morty & Me

MIMI SHERMAN

CHAPTER 3

What Activities Did You Engage in for Entertainment?

When I was a young girl, we didn't have a TV, and we just listened to the radio. We went to the movies, but that seemed a little farfetched from where I lived and did. I didn't see how affluent people lived or how the middle class lived. Today, we see and know everything! The world has become an open book. We did not have a car. Our means of transportation was the train or very occasionally a bus. I remember my friend Gilda lived in a two-bedroom apartment, her father had a car, and I considered them to be rich! Everyone I knew lived the way I did.

On Saturday morning, Morty and I were not allowed to meet our friends or go to a movie, etc., until we completed our chores in the apartment. I would dust all the furniture, and Morty would carpet sweep. We did not have a vacuum cleaner. My mother would hand-wash and scrub all the clothing and bedsheets and hang everything on a clothesline outside the window of our building to dry. Then she would clean the kitchen and bathroom. We sang songs, and my mother listened to opera on the radio while we worked. On Sunday, she would cook several meals for the week. We never ate out or ordered food in.

My father did not help. Men in those days were under the impression that this was woman's work, and men were not allowed to engage in cleaning. How fortunate for them that they instituted that law. How lucky for married people today that it doesn't exist anymore!

When we went outside, we played all sorts of games on the sidewalk and in the street in front of our building. Few cars were parked there, and very few cars drove by. Everyone was included. Age did not matter nor did your gender. On the sidewalk, we played jacks, pickup sticks, king against the wall, and hopscotch. In the street, we played stickball, matched baseball cards, played marbles, played punch-ball, etc.

We went roller-skating and bicycle riding on weekends when we could afford to. Bronx Park was about six blocks from where we lived. We picnicked there and played handball and paddle tennis. In the winter, we went ice-skating and sleigh riding at Bronx Park. We were completely frozen by the time we left the park and had to walk home.

We listened to the radio constantly. My favorite programs were *The Shadow*, *The Lone Ranger*, *The Goldbergs*, and *Inner Sanctum*. I remember how scared everyone was when Orson Welles's show called "The War of The Worlds" was broadcast. It was so real that it caused a nationwide panic!

People were talking about this new form of entertainment called television. There was a radio store on the main street near where I lived. Everyone came to see this little box that showed a movie. There were rows and rows of people staring through the windows of the store, including me. In 1948, my parents bought a large console with a small TV in it—about 8" by 10". TVs at that time were only black-and-white. Color TVs were then available in the 1950s. We loved watching this new TV; and some of our favorite shows were *The Milton Berle Show*, *The Sid Caesar Show*, and *Your Show of Shows*.

On one occasion, during Easter vacation, when I was only twelve years old, my mother allowed me to take my brother, who was eight years old, and my two cousins, who were seven and ten, to see a movie downtown. We traveled for one hour by train to 42nd Street, had lunch at the automat—a new concept in restaurants—and then went to Radio City Music Hall to see a movie. After the movie, we traveled by train during rush hour back to where we lived. Come to think of it, I was only twelve and had to assume these huge responsibilities of seven-, eight-, and ten-year-old children. This would never happen today!

CHAPTER 4

What Do You Remember from Your Childhood That You Would Never Want to Relive Again?

When I was about six or seven years old, we lived in a Jewish neighborhood in a small apartment. It was 1934–35. The country was in a terrible depression, and my parents could not find any jobs. As a result, they were unable to pay the rent for their apartment. The landlord waited one month, two months, and then three months. He threatened to evict them! I came home from school one day and found all the furniture and clothes and whatever we had on the sidewalk in front of our building. I started to cry. I was much too young to understand the full circumstances of what had happened. We had no place to go! Family and friends lived in small apartments, and they were struggling as well. I had to go to one place, my mother to another, etc.

My parents finally found an apartment in an Italian neighborhood, which was quite far from the subway station and less expensive. The new building did not have an elevator. We had to walk up three flights to get to our apartment. Everyone accepted us. I became friendly with some ladies in the building. They fed me pasta with a wonderful sauce on it whereas my mother made spaghetti with ketchup. It was delicious! We lived there for several years, and when I was a little older, these kind women taught me how to knit and crochet. I didn't appreciate it then, but this skill became an important part of my life.

I played with all the children in the neighborhood. There was a famous church at the end of the block where we played very often. One day, when I was about eleven years old, a group of boys—who were my friends—accused me and my family of killing Jesus Christ because we were Jewish. They were about to beat me up, but I had anticipated it and ran away for dear life. However, my brother who was only seven was beaten unmercifully. My parents decided that we must move to a Jewish area . . . which we did!

We had been living in the new neighborhood for over a year when our whole apartment caught fire. Everything in the apartment was ruined, the furniture, clothing, my piano, etc. Once again, we had to find a place to stay and sleep for several weeks while the apartment was repaired. And once again, we had to be separated. We had to buy all new furniture and clothing and basic home necessities. My mother asked me if I wanted to continue with piano lessons. We had a piano, and I had taken lessons for more than a year, if I continued, they would have to buy a piano. The original one was destroyed in the fire. I felt so bad about the money that they were spending. Therefore, I didn't want them to incur additional expenses for me. I said no, and years later, I was so sorry that I had made that decision.

CHAPTER 5

How Did Your Parents Feel about You Wanting to Go to College?

Money was always an issue. When I graduated from high school, I was sixteen and a half. I felt that I was too young to work at that point. Although most of my friends went to work, I told my parents I wanted to go to college. I was the first member of my family to go to college. My mother had two brothers and a sister, all of whom had their own families. My father had a brother who was married with two children. No one had gone to college; they all worked.

When I told my parents that I wanted to go to college, I told them I would continue to work so it wouldn't cost them anything. As it turned out, I received a scholarship to City College Uptown. The result was it didn't cost me anything either. I worked every summer as a waitress at beautiful hotels in upper New York State. I also got a job in the library at the college. This afforded me daily spending money and the opportunity to do research for various class projects. As a matter of fact, I had been working since I was fourteen.

On August 9, 1945, while I was working as a waitress at an adult camp, I heard that World War II ended. I was overjoyed and motivated to write the following letter.

Dear Dad, Mom, and Morty,

I know that you, mom, and Morty won't be home to receive this letter, but I want you all to know how I feel and what has happened these past few hours.

I woke up this morning at the usual hour of 7:30, jumped out of bed, slipped into my clothes, and ran to the bathroom to get washed. On my way to the dining room, I heard a commotion in the lifeguards' room. I ran in and heard the wonderful, marvelous news over the radio. World War II is over! I ran up to the dining room and started jumping around like a crazy one. I was so happy. I told everyone, and at first, they didn't believe me, but as each person came up to the dining room with the news, they gradually began to believe it.

We all realized it wasn't confirmed, but it's at least one step forward. When the guests came in, the dining room was in an uproar! The fellows put lipstick on their fingers and started pinching all the guests and girls. I was serving breakfast with lipstick all over my face.

My guests couldn't eat much. One lady cried, and everyone else had tears in their eyes. I can't actually describe how things really looked.

I feel elated as if a great load was lifted from my brain, and yet I haven't any sisters or brothers over there. I have a few cousins who are in, and they are going to school. If I who have no one feel this way, can you imagine how those who have someone feel? And what about those who have sons who died for this? They are the ones who suffer while everyone else is rejoicing.

My first thought was that I'd like to be with my family, not alone with strangers, for this is a moment I'll always remember. I immediately thought I'd like to go into New York and go downtown and yell and scream at the top of my lungs. I'd like to go into all the restaurants and movie houses (since everything will be free), but most of all, I'd like to be with you. It's funny that I should feel so sentimental.

Another thought just struck me. Do you realize that I don't really know what a peaceful world is like? I matured in a war, and what was before is quite vague. What is it like without seeing headlines in the newspapers about war and hearing commentators talking about something besides war? I just can't imagine it. What is it like to see boys in civilian clothes, no uniforms, no nothing?

I can't write much more. I'm in one of those moods. Gee, how I miss you and love you all. Everyone sends their best regards. Love and kisses.

With all my love,
Mimi

PS Please save this letter.

MIMI SHERMAN

CHAPTER 6

How Did the Students and Professors Treat You?

City College Uptown was located at 145th Street and Amsterdam Avenue. This meant that I had to take the train to 59th Street in Manhattan and transfer to another train that went uptown to 145th Street. It took one and a half hours to get there and even longer during the rush hour. When I was able to obtain a seat, I spent my time studying or reading. It was basically a boys' college, and these boys were the smartest in New York. They were from the High School of Math and Science or from other high schools of that caliber. The college had just opened their enrollment to females with the provision that they graduate with an education degree.

I really wasn't happy about it because I was mingling with very bright males, and they were majoring in engineering and medicine. I wanted to do that too, and everybody laughed at me and said, "Ha Ha, you're a girl. You can't go into those fields." Since I was very good in math, I decided to become a math teacher. The classes that I took consisted of all boys. I was the only female in the class. The other females that I met there were all going for elementary education. They were not interested in teaching on the secondary level where you had to major in a subject.

I finally took a physics class, which was a requirement for the math teacher license. My physics professor said in front of the entire class, "Miss Fleshler (that was my maiden name), what grade do you think you are going to receive in this class?" I shrugged my shoulders and whispered, "I think that I should receive an A. I have gotten high marks in all of my exams." He answered, "If you think that you are going to get an A, then you are mistaken. I don't give girls A's." And you know what happened? I never got that A, and I really deserved it. I got a B+. Today, that man would have been fired and rightfully so. That was how women were treated back then! They were second-class citizens! We have achieved a great deal in the last seventy-five years.

The boys that were in most of my classes admired the fact that I was smart enough to keep up with them and sometimes surpass them. Most of the professors were decent, but a few were intolerable!

CHAPTER 7

What Were Your Parents' Political Views and How Did Joining a Union Affect Their Lives?

My father was a very socialistic and communistic guy. He would go to union meetings on Friday nights. There were men outside of the meeting place who opposed joining a union for painters. These men would try to interrupt the meeting. A physical fight would occur, and many times, my father would come home with bruises all over his face and body. He felt so strongly about the establishment of a union because the union promised to fight for many benefits that workers did not have. These included hospitalization, higher wages, a two-week vacation, a shorter workday, and overall better conditions in the workplace. Through the years, these items have become federal laws. He continued to go to these meetings to fight for what he believed in!

My mother too would try to convince people to join the union. I remember that the whole family would travel by train down to Manhattan on May Day, which was May 1, to march in a parade. We were marching to make life easier for the worker. We marched for hours, chanting songs that dealt with improving working conditions.

On the other hand, my friend had a factory in lower Manhattan where he manufactured low-priced women's sportswear. It was a nonunion shop and perhaps considered to be a sweatshop. He was doing very well financially. A garment industry union organizer came to his place of business and demanded that the workers join the union. He, in turn, refused! He did not want a union shop for many reasons, one of which was he thought he would lose control of his own business. He was continually harassed and threatened by the garment workers union. In addition, irreparable associates of the union demanded protection money unless he agreed to allow his employees to join the union.

It finally reached a point where he had had enough. He told his wife and kids that they were leaving New York and moving to Florida now. He closed his business and left in a few days. He started a similar business in South Florida, was not harassed by anyone, and was quite happy and successful.

Not far from where I lived, there was a group of apartment buildings called the "Cooperatives." Most of the people who lived there were known to be socialists or communists. They would invite outsiders to their meetings to try to convert them to their beliefs. My father would attend some of their meetings. He never signed anything that would make him a member of the "Socialist Party" or the "Communist Party." Thank goodness! When McCarthy was in power in the 1950s and '60s, many of these people were arrested and convicted.

In 1952, I applied for a math teaching position at Forest Hills High School. Before they could give me the position, I had to sign a paper that said that I am not a member of the Communist Party. Of course, I signed it and got the job. At the same time, all the teachers at all the schools in New York had to sign this paper.

There was a very fine math teacher, who had been at this high school for many a very long time, who refused to sign the paper. He was fired. Those were terrible times!

Mom, Dad, Morty & Me

CHAPTER 8

What Kind of Social Life Did You Have As a Teenager and As a Young Adult?

My social life as a teenager was very limited. It consisted of going with my girlfriends to a friend's house that had a basement. We would meet a group of teenage boys and dance the night away. We loved to do the Lindy . . . jitterbug. There was never any food, alcohol, or drinks served. There was little or no romance. We just loved to dance and practice new steps. There were times, however, when we would meet at Bronx Park and play spin the bottle.

When I was thirteen, my parents decided to send me to a sleepaway camp for two weeks. It was during World War II, and my parents were earning more money. It was a German camp, but my parents did not know that initially. The girls in my bunk were older than me and loved to talk about sex. I had no knowledge of anything related to sex. They did not teach it at school, and my parents were too embarrassed to talk to me about it. When I went to the movies, and there were love scenes, only kissing was allowed then. The girls teased me because I was Jewish and laughed at me because I was so ignorant. They decided to explain to me what sexual intercourse was about. I could not believe that my parents would engage in this activity. I could not sleep that night! When I returned home, I confronted my mother and aunt, who was visiting, about sex. They said that what these girls told me about sex was not true, and they refused to discuss it further. My mother did apologize for sending me there. She did not know that it was a German camp.

Although I was in contact with lots of boys in college, most of them were nerdy, and I was completely disinterested in them. There was one boy who was brilliant, and I spent some time with him studying and working on homework. I was not attracted to him at all. He, on the other hand, was very attracted to me. However, I was not aware of it. That summer, I worked as a waitress at the Commodore Hotel near Poughkeepsie, New York. I started dating the lifeguard who was very handsome and charming and in demand by many girls and young women who were there for the summer. His name was Sid, and I was very flattered that he was interested in me. The brilliant college boy heard about it, was exceedingly jealous, and came to the hotel to kill the lifeguard. He had a knife with him. Luckily, I managed to talk him out of killing anyone and the consequences that would occur. I also explained to him that we were never romantically involved. Not such a brilliant boy after all!

I was nineteen at the time and had completed three years of college. When the summer was over, I returned to my parents' home in the Bronx. Sid returned to his home in Brooklyn. We continued seeing each other, but it was difficult. We often met in Manhattan. After two months, Sid proposed to me and gave me a lovely engagement ring. However, things did not work out for us, and we terminated our relationship. Yes, I did return the engagement ring.

As a young adult, I would meet my girlfriends, Gilda, Trudy, and Sherry, who were single, and go down to Manhattan to a hotel that had advertised a dance in the newspaper. Most of my other friends were married by the time they were twenty. Occasionally, we would meet a guy but mostly not.

When I graduated from college, I no longer had to work as a waitress during the summer. My three friends and I decided to rent an apartment in Long Beach, over an hour from where we lived, for July and August. This was an outrageous thing to do because we all lived with our parents. In those days, you were considered a loose woman if you moved out and got your own apartment. If you had a boyfriend and moved in together, it was unheard of; and again, you would be considered a "Tramp." We all begged our parents to allow us to do this. We were all working and had saved enough money to afford it. During the day, we went to the beach to get the darkest suntan possible. My friends would sit with a reflector, iodine, and olive oil to get the best sunburn. I just used suntan lotion. Years later, it was determined that using the above caused cancer. I was so happy that I never used those products! I was a little bored just going to the beach every day, so I decided to get a part-time job in town. I did get one as a salesgirl at a ladies' clothing store. I learned about style, which helped me create my own style. At night, we went to the Nassau Hotel, which was on the boardwalk, to party. This was the place to be seen! It was very informal and lots of fun!

CHAPTER 9

How Did You Learn How to Sew, Knit, and Crochet?

My mother wore a plus-size dress. The plus-size dresses in the stores looked like housedresses and were ugly. She would bring home patterns and fabric from the factory. She worked for firms that sold very expensive dresses. She was the sample maker. She sewed the new style dresses together, which were shown to the buyers who came to the "garment center" to buy clothes for the stores they worked for. She was very talented! The owner of the firm rewarded her by giving her the patterns and fabric without charging her.

She would enlarge the pattern for herself and change the pattern slightly for me. We had a Singer sewing machine, which she used to sew our dresses together. I was her assistant. I had to finish everything, the hem, the buttonholes, and the buttons. I hated wearing these dresses, but I had nothing else to wear. All my friends wore store-bought clothes, and I wanted to do that too. When I was sixteen years old, I had saved enough money to buy some clothes at a store. That was a happy day! Learning how to finish clothing helped me greatly when I got older. However, my mother never allowed me to use the sewing machine, and she would not teach me how to use it for fear that I would break it. One day, when my mother was working and I was home alone, I decided to learn how to sew on the machine. I did learn how, and that knowledge also helped me in future years.

When I was seventeen, I asked my mother whether I could visit her where she worked. She agreed, and I took the train to 34th Street in Manhattan. I walked to 37th Street and then to Eighth Avenue. There were men hanging around, and some were loading and unloading trucks. When they saw me, they started calling me names, using obscene language, and propositioning me. I felt very embarrassed and demeaned! Since then, these men have been advised that if they continue this behavior, they would be arrested. Their behavior has changed considerably!

When I got to my mother's factory, I could not believe the conditions these poor people had to work under. There were rows and rows of men and women, sitting, sweaty, and bent over their sewing machines. The air was foggy and hot due to the huge pressing machines that were needed to press all the dresses produced. There were no air conditioners then. They did have some fans blowing, but the fans were blowing hot air. The workers had to tolerate these conditions. There was no alternative. I really felt sorry for my mother!

Small Crocheted Evening Bags

CHAPTER 10

What Did Your Parents Think of President Roosevelt, and What Effect Did the Holocaust Have on Your Family?

They loved President Roosevelt! We listened to his speeches on the radio and discussed everything afterward. We thought that he was very kind to the Jewish people but discovered years later that he was not. During the Holocaust, a ship arrived from Germany filled with Jewish families. They were told they would be admitted to this country. However, President Roosevelt did not allow them entry and sent them back to Germany. Back in Germany, they were exterminated. What a horror! When Roosevelt died, we did not think much of President Truman. However, he was a good friend to the Jewish people. He was partly responsible for the establishment of the State of Israel.

In the 1930s and '40s during the Holocaust, people in this country had no idea about the six million Jews and other nationalities being slaughtered in Germany. We listened to the news on the radio and read the *New York Times* and the *Forward* but knew very little. I don't think our government was aware of this either.

My mother had lived in a ghetto in Lublin, Poland. Polish men would come to the ghetto and accost the women there. They would burn down their houses and treat them very poorly. My mother worked at home, and her father would not allow her and her sisters to read or write. She worked at a very early age and gave her wages to her father. My mother finally came to this country in 1923 for a better life. My father also lived in Lublin but did not know her. His father was very religious. My father hated going to Hebrew school. His father was a tyrant. As an example, one day my father overslept, and his father brought a pail of ice-cold water into his room and poured it all over my father. At another time, my father left Hebrew school early with some of his friends. His father went after him, picked my father up high in the air, and tossed him onto the cement sidewalk. He was bloody and bruised afterward.

It was World War I, and Russia now occupied Lublin. My father was forced to go into the Russian army. After some training, he heard that they were sending his unit to the front where all the fighting was. My father was afraid that he would be killed there, so he decided to escape. The next morning, his unit was put on a train that was heading to the front. At a turn, the train slowed down, and he jumped off the train and ran for his life. He hitched his way to Paris and then London. His brother, who lived in the United States, had to sign a lot of documents and send a great deal of money to get my father passage on a ship that was going to New York. He arrived at Ellis Island in 1920.

In 1926, the people who had immigrate'd here from Lublin, Poland, decided to have a reunion party, which they called a banquet. My mother and father met at this party. My mother had a lovely voice, and she would entertain everyone by singing Jewish songs. Her favorite was "A Yiddisha Mama." They were married in 1927, and I was born a year later.

The Holocaust was devastating for my family. My mother had a brother, sister, and father who remained in Lublin. Her brother and sister were married, and each had two children. They were all sent to concentration camps and murdered! She also had three siblings who lived near us in the Bronx and were married with children. Her mother had left Poland as well and lived with us. My father's father remained there and ultimately met his death. My father's sister had moved to Israel, and his brother lived near us in the Bronx. He was married with two children.

This was a heart-wrenching experience for our entire family!

CHAPTER 11

What Teaching Positions Did You Have After You Received Your College Degree?

I graduated from City College in 1949. It was difficult to get a job because all the boys were returning from serving in World War II, and they were getting the teaching jobs. However, my cousin knew the principal of a school in Manhattan on 109th Street and Amsterdam Avenue. This was a very poor neighborhood in those days, consisting of Afro-Americans, Hispanics, and Irish. I was to teach eighth-grade math, which was difficult for me because I was basically a high school teacher.

Our society was completely unaware of what was happening in some of our schools. Everything unsavory was swept under the carpet. At this school, fire trucks and ambulances were at the school constantly. Two teachers were beaten up by some incorrigible students and sent to the hospital. Sex was engaged in the hallway closets; and sexual drawings of students and teachers, including me, were on the walls of the hallways!

I remember going to one of the tenements to speak to a child's parent because he brought a knife to class. I was very young and naive. There was trash in the hallway of the building. I climbed up four flights to get to the parents' apartment, and the smell was nauseating. When I finally reached his mother, she said that she was unable to do anything with her son. She said, "You handle him and don't bother me." I was completely devastated and felt foolish that I had gone to see her. That was the one and only visit I ever made!

These parents were disinterested and uninvolved. I felt threatened every day in school and after school. I had to walk several blocks all alone to the train station. I was always afraid that some students would attack me. I taught there for one semester and then left. I was so relieved that I did not have to go there anymore! I felt that, perhaps, teaching is not for me.

In the 1950s, the movie *Blackboard Jungle* was released. People became aware of the difficulties that existed when one had to teach in a poor neighborhood. Young men and women just out of college are sent to these schools, and some never continue as a teacher because of a similar bad experience.

After one week relaxing at home, I received a call from the chairman of the math department at Christopher Columbus High School, my alma mater. I had done student teaching there the previous year and learned more about teaching than all the education classes that I had to take at college for my teaching license. He offered me a teaching position for one month. The original teacher had to have surgery.

I was upset to see that one of the students in my geometry class was my brother, Morty. He was very obnoxious to me and threatened to create a disturbance in the class every day. He thought he was very funny! I complained to my mother but to no avail. I could not possibly complain to my father. My father would get his wide, heavy belt and beat Morty as he had done in the past. Parents no longer are allowed to hit their children. If reported, they could be arrested.

After three weeks, the chairman informed me that I must administer tests to all my classes because the teacher was returning shortly. I spent hours creating all these tests. There was no way that I would allow my brother to see the test in advance. I even slept with them under my pillow. I hated Morty at this moment!

Guess who got the highest grade in the class. That's right . . . Morty! The students, all commented, "Of course, he got the highest grade. The teacher is his sister." To his credit, Morty was very smart! He went on to get bachelor's, master's, and doctorate degrees at Penn State University.

Apparently, this teaching experience got me positions at Evander Childs High School in the Bronx and then Forest Hills High School and Long Island City High School in Queens, New York. Teachers would go on sabbatical leave, and I would replace them for one year. I was called a permanent substitute.

CHAPTER 12

How Did You Meet Your Husband, and What Followed?

One day, in Long Beach, I was at the beach lying on a blanket, basking in the sun, and reading a book when a guy tried to involve me in conversation. He was tall and handsome, but I thought that he was too flirtatious. Therefore, I did not respond in a friendly manner. That Saturday night, my roommate Trudi and I decided to go to the opening dance at the new Capri Beach Club in Atlantic Beach. She stopped to talk to a guy she knew, and with him was that guy who had tried to "pick me up." We were formally introduced. His name was Bob, he was going to law school, and his parents rented an apartment in Long Beach. They lived in the Bronx, on the Grand Concourse, near Yankee Stadium. That was a beautiful area, much nicer than where I lived.

We danced, talked, and enjoyed each other's company. We dated on and off for the next few months. Then Bob asked me for a date on New Year's Eve. It was 1950–51. That night, we determined that our relationship was more than a casual one. We started dating seriously, and we were now boyfriend and girlfriend! What endeared me to Bob—more than anything else—was his love for babies. He was an only child and always wanted a sibling. When we walked on the boardwalk or in town, he had to stop at every carriage to admire the baby. This was encouraged then but is almost prohibited today for fear of transmitting a disease to the baby or the possibility of a kidnapping!

Bob attended New York Law School and was very busy with classes, homework, and studying. I was busy as well, teaching and attending New York University for my master's degree. I needed one to teach on the secondary level in New York City. We dated on weekends. It was difficult to go from the West Bronx to where I lived using mass transportation. He was able to borrow his father's car, which was a light blue Cadillac Convertible. All the neighbors were amazed, and so was I. I had never seen such a beautiful car!

There were no cell phones, and we did not have a phone. My neighbor had a phone, and she was kind enough to let me use it. I would give her telephone number to anyone who wanted to call me. It was a difficult situation for her. She was an elderly woman. She had to go out in the hallway to ring my bell, to tell me that there was a call for me. My parents finally agreed to buy a phone.

My friends and I rented the same apartment in Long Beach the following summer. Bob's parents (Mabel and Irving) had also rented, in a much better location, in Long Beach. Bob and I saw each other every day and night. At the end of the summer, we decided to walk to the end of the boardwalk. He told me that he loved me, proposed marriage, and gave me a beautiful two-carat diamond ring. I was very emotional! I had not expected this at all. I told him that the feeling was mutual.

His parents were very comfortable. They lived in a large and beautifully furnished apartment. His mother had completed high school and wore expensive clothing and jewelry. His father was a dentist and did very well. They had aspirations that their only son would marry a girl from a rich family, not a poor girl with immigrant parents. Notwithstanding, I was well educated and able to support myself. On the other hand, Bob had never had a job.

Since we were now engaged, my parents felt that they had to invite his parents for dinner. My father set up a long rectangular table in the living room. My mother bought new table linens and tried to set a beautiful table. She made her usual delicious food, and surprisingly, my mother and mother-in-law got along very well. Rose and Mabel, who would have imagined this! She loved my mother's Jewish food. I had had such trepidation that something would go wrong because they came from two different worlds.

They discussed arranging a wedding. Bob's parents insisted that the wedding be held at a fancy hotel in Manhattan. My parents offered to contribute what they could afford. They gave much more than I thought they had. We were married at the Royal Plaza Hotel, which was across the street from the famous Plaza Hotel, in June 1952. My family and friends, who were at the wedding, had never seen anything like it. They could not get over the people, the clothes, the jewelry, the liquor, and the food! They were very impressed! We were the "talk of Allerton Avenue" where we all lived!

CHAPTER 13

How Were You Affected by Your Parents' Divorce?

There were no air conditioners then, and it could be brutally hot in the summer where we lived. There were times when we slept on the fire escape outside our kitchen window just to get a little air. My mother decided to rent a small apartment in Far Rockaway for July and August. It was 1941, and she was making more money so they could afford it. It was near the Atlantic Ocean. We took a special train from Manhattan to get there, and my parents had to use this train to go to work and to return in the evening. The trip took one and a half hours.

It was rare for women to earn more than their husbands. My mother was earning more than my father, and this led to a lot of arguments. They quarreled a great deal about money because she was working so hard, and he was often unemployed. One day, my mother asked me to take a walk with her. After ten minutes, we found a bench and rested. She said, "I would like to talk to you about something." I was thirteen years old and thought that I did something to upset her. She said, "I would like to divorce your father." I was completely stunned! Nobody ever got a divorce then. It would be terribly embarrassing for my family and friends. These thoughts were running through my mind, and I started to cry. With constant tears running down my face, I begged my mother to reconsider because it would be a "Shanda" (shame) for everyone. She did reconsider, unfortunately, and they lived together miserably for the next ten years.

When I was twenty-three years old, I got married and was on my honeymoon when my father packed his belongings and moved out. For the last few months, he had been experiencing "Petit Mal Epilepsy Fits." This was very dangerous to his health. The doctor felt that they were due to the stress at home and advised him to leave. My father never had any more epileptic fits. The doctor was correct in his diagnosis. Five years later, he married a lovely woman named Claire. His life was less stressful, and as a result, he was happy and healthy.

My brother, who was only nineteen, was affected by the divorce and the fact that I no longer lived at home. My mother was unhappy, and she was constantly talking about the divorce. They could not be invited to the same event, and she was angry when we went to see him. She was not interested in marriage. I was married and had a new life in Queens, so I was not as affected as much as Morty. He eventually left home and joined the Army.

CHAPTER 14

How Was Married Life at First?

We rented a one-bedroom apartment in a new building in Rego Park. I was teaching at Long Island City High School when I found out that I was pregnant. In those days, you were not allowed to teach beyond the fifth month if you were pregnant. Today, you can teach until you have the child. I had to resign! A few weeks later, my leg swelled to twice its size, and I could not walk. I ended up in the hospital. I had phlebitis, which is a blood clot in the veins of the leg. At that time, the only drug available was penicillin. They kept me there for one week for fear that the clot would travel to my heart. When I was finally released, I had to wear a rubber stocking for one year. Medical care was quite different in those days.

Richard (Rick) was born on July 13, 1954. My husband was so happy the baby was a boy. He now had his own baby to play with. Two and a half years later, on February 11, 1957, Carol was born. I was so happy to have a daughter. I would meet my friend at the corner luncheonette with the baby in a large carriage and park the carriage outside with the baby asleep in it. She did the same thing. We would take the two older toddlers inside. Think of it! Two babies left outside alone! No fear of anything! Of course, we checked on the babies constantly, but today, you would be arrested and rightfully so!

The apartment became very crowded. Bob's parents and grandparents, whom he was very close to, decided to buy us a house. We found a dream split-level house in North Woodmere, Long Island, New York, for $24,000. I was in heaven! I had never seen anything so beautiful! I could not believe how lucky I was! Bob had to leave his law clerk job because it paid so little. He got a job as an insurance adjuster.

My job was to take care of the children and house. I met Janet, who lived around the corner, and we bonded. She was an artist, had been a teacher also, and had three young children. We could not afford a landscaper, so we decided to do what our neighbors paid a lot of money for. We built a marble retaining wall at my house and at her house. We chiseled the marble; mixed cement powder, sand, and water; and built a wall across the front of our houses. Men would park their cars in front of my house to watch us work. We were wearing shorts and tank tops, and there were five little kids playing with the cement mixture in a wheel barrel. I also got Bob, Morty, and my dad to break up a cement straight path and, with my help, to build a marble curved path. We were only thirty years old and had a lot of energy. We also tried to improve the decor of the inside of the house. We painted walls and furniture, and Janet drew a mural in my dining room. We were very productive young women who did unusual things while mothering toddlers.

My mother decided to give me her Singer sewing machine because she wasn't using it anymore. I began by sewing little dresses for my daughter and then mother-and-daughter matching dresses. People thought that I should go into business; the dresses were so cute. But I knew nothing about business. I liked to be busy and began to knit and crochet while I watched TV in the evening.

In 1963, I became pregnant again. Rick was almost nine, and Carol was seven. And they helped diaper, bathe, and feed Bruce, born on November 28, 1963. He was their new and best toy! We almost felt like they were the parents, and we were the grandparents. He responded well to all of us.

My brother returned from the Army, met Helen, and married her a few years later after they both got their doctorates. We became very close. We spent all holidays together and had similar interests socially. She was not like a sister-in-law but more like a sister. They had three children, Steven, Lauren, and Glenn. Their family now includes Mayumi, Jocelyn, and grandson Nathaniel.

My Wedding Picture

Bob's Parents

CHAPTER 15

What Was It like Going Back to Teaching?

I joined the PTA at the elementary school that Carol and Rick attended. It was a very active PTA with lots of fundraising events. There was an election, and I was voted as president. I was very busy, and my phone did not stop ringing, especially at dinnertime. My husband was a male chauvinist, and through these last few years, he was opposed to me returning to teaching. We certainly needed the money, but he felt that a woman's place is in the home. He was so annoyed with the amount of time I was spending away from the family and particularly from him that he said, "You might as well get a job and make some money." I retorted, "You mean a teaching job?" He said, "Yes." I was happy about that. The principal of the junior high school had recently contacted me about teaching part time. Bruce was now almost three, and I sent him to nursery school while I taught two algebra classes and one honors geometry class. I loved the arrangement. This lasted until Bruce entered first grade. They needed a full-time math teacher now, and I agreed.

Carol and Rick went to this junior high school. There were times that it was a little difficult for them and for me. Kids would talk about me in front of them. Perhaps it was to say that they liked or did not like what I wore that day. They were somewhat embarrassed. Of course, it could be something worse. At times, they acknowledged me in the hallway with a smile, hand motion, or "Hello, Mrs. Sherman." They often complained about a teacher they had, whom I was friendly with. There was nothing that I could do. They were annoyed!

In New York State, a Regents test is given for ninth and tenth-grade math, as well as many other subjects. It was required that you take Regents classes to apply to a good college. At the junior high school, final tests were given at the end of the school year. In my classes, if you received 100% or 99% on the Regents or the final, you were invited to my home for a celebration, which included dinner. It was a great incentive for students to try harder, and some really did. They would come for extra help at the end of the day until they mastered the subject. One year, I had thirty-three students who achieved 100% or 99% for dinner. We did not think of bringing in food at that time. Yes, I did the cooking. Crazy, isn't it?

In 1980, the junior high school, which consisted of seventh, eighth, and ninth grades, would now become Woodmere Middle School. The ninth grade moved to the high school, and the sixth grade became part of the middle-school. I decided to remain at the middle-school because it was closer to my home and less stressful than the demands that I would have at Hewlett High School. However, I had to teach eighth-grade math. Fortunately, the curriculum here was much more advanced than what I taught years ago. It included a lot of algebra and even some geometry that were considered high school topics when I went to school. There were also enriched and advanced classes that I taught. After school hours, I tutored some students to supplement our income.

One day, a boy ran into my room to tell me that *a student* had a gun. I thanked him and told him that I will take care of it. When *the student* sat down at his desk, I quietly walked over to him and asked him if he had a gun in his possession. He first hesitated to answer me, but I reassured him that I would put it in a drawer and return it to him when the period was over. He gave me the gun! I put it in a desk drawer and proceeded to teach the lesson that I had prepared. My practice was to give the students an example to work on while I generally would walk around the room to help those students who needed an individual explanation. I quietly asked the initial informant to go to the office and tell the vice principal or the guidance counselors about the gun. Two minutes later, they all walked into my classroom. They removed *the student* from class, and I handed them the gun. I continued to teach the lesson as if nothing had transpired.

That afternoon, I received a message to report to the principal's office. I thought that she wanted to hear the story about the gun from me. Instead, she informed me that I must be there tomorrow morning at 7:30 to meet with *the student's* father, who is very wealthy and powerful. I was not intimidated because I felt that I had handled the problem correctly. When I got to the school the next morning, there was a huge black limousine in front of the school. I met *the student's* father in the principal's office. He started to yell at me for embarrassing his son, and he said, "I'm going to go to the school board and bring you up on charges for mistreating my son." I said, " Mr.—, your son brought a gun to school, which is illegal, and furthermore, I have the best reputation in this school. There is a waiting list of students who want to be in my class. I don't think that you would be very successful with charges." He did not say another word and stormed out of the office. All the teachers had a lot to talk about that week!

CHAPTER 16

How Important Was Tennis to Your Family?

How Did You Start Your Sweater Business?

Bob, my husband, loved to play tennis; and his mood for the day was determined by how he played that day. Rick and Bruce were also very good tennis players, and they made the tennis team in high school. Carol was not interested but played squash instead. Ironically, Carol is a tennis player today. Back then, I had just learned to play tennis, and I played poorly.

In 1977, we joined the Atlantic Beach tennis club, which entitled us to a locker at the beach as well. We were able to afford this because Bob had recently bought a liquor store in Wall Street—with the help of his family. I managed to play tennis with people who were on my level. That is where I met Ilene, who became my best friend, my tennis partner, and very influential in my life.

I spent my days at Atlantic Beach playing tennis, having lunch, swimming, socializing, and knitting. I had just completed a ribbon sweater for my mother-in-law and brought it to show the ladies. One lady said, "I would love to buy it. How much do you want for it?" I had no intention of selling the sweater to her, and I told her so nicely. Ilene poked me in the ribs and said, "Sell it to her. You'll make another one." I did not know what to charge her for the sweater. I tried to calculate the cost of the ribbon, the time I spent making it, and the profit. I thought if I asked a ridiculously high price, she would say no. I said, "One hundred dollars." She said, "I'll take it." After she paid me, Ilene said to me, "You should knit five sample sweaters and sell them to the boutique stores. You can make a lot of money." The word "money" was the incentive!

I designed and knitted five ribbon sweaters in different colors and in different styles and patterns, including angora and mohair. I brought them to four boutiques in Cedarhurst and Woodmere and to Tango in Roslyn. Each store ordered twenty sweaters in different colors and styles. This was unusual for a boutique store because their customers paid a lot of money to own a one-of-a-kind sweater. They didn't want anyone else wearing the same sweater.

It was the beginning of August, and school started in one month. There wasn't any way that I could knit one hundred sweaters! I advertised in the local Penny-saver for knitters who would like to make extra money working at home. They were to come to my house on a specific date to show me sweaters that they had knitted. I had written up instructions and drew a diagram for each sweater. I assembled yarn in bags with the instructions and handed them out to those women that I hired. I consulted with each knitter to further explain the front, back, and sleeves and used the diagram to simplify it. A picture is worth a thousand words! I hired a woman who sewed the front and back together and then sewed the sleeves in. I had someone press the sweaters—block them. Someone else added beading and all kinds of trimmings to the sweaters. The most important person that I hired was a sales rep. She helped me deliver the sweaters, and she would get orders for more. This was called a "cottage industry," and at one point, I had twenty women working for me!

School started, and I was the busiest person! Imagine this; I taught five classes. I marked five sets of math homework each night because I thought it was important to do. It reinforced what I taught that day. I had a lot of success with students who had not done well in math previously. I did not want to change that. The knitters would come to my house after school or on weekends to bring the pieces that they knitted. They also called me at all hours when they had problems with the directions. I paid them and gave them a new sweater to knit. I checked each sweater very carefully. I was a perfectionist with these sweaters! There were many nights when I was up 'til three in the morning redoing something that was not right. I named the company "Mimi Originals" and ordered labels, cards, and billing paraphernalia.

When I accumulated some sweaters, I would bring them to the lady who sewed them together, or she would pick them up instead. Then I would take them to the blocker and then to the trimming lady. Bruce would sometimes help me with deliveries. When they were completed, I brought them to my sales rep, who mailed them to the stores. I would spend many afternoons traveling to Manhattan or Brooklyn to buy yarn and trimmings. To add to all of this, I had a husband and Bruce at home, who needed my attention. Thankfully, Carol and Rick were in college. I also made dinner for the family every night. When I think about this period in my life today, I don't know how I did it all!

After one month, I realized I had many bills to pay, and I didn't have the money to pay them. Besides paying the ladies who knitted and finished the sweaters, I also had to pay the yarn companies and the companies that supplied the trimming material, as well my sales rep. The boutiques that I sold to were very often late in paying their bills. I decided to borrow money from the local bank. I conferred with the vice president of the bank and requested a loan of $10,000. He approved the loan after hearing about my sweater business. Then he told me that I would have to pay 21 percent interest on the loan. I was upset! I never heard of such a high interest rate! I calculated what it would cost me, and I was furious. I even thought that they were taking advantage of me because I was a woman. I was in a very difficult situation! I desperately needed the loan, so I decided to accept his offer. Fortunately, all of the outstanding bills from the boutiques were paid within a few weeks; and I was able to pay the loan back, which incurred much less interest.

I continued to design more beautiful sweaters. At night, I would dream of different designs and would have to jot them down, or I might forget them in the morning. I extended my sweater business into lace skirts that can be worn with the sweaters. I made a sweater set where the sleeves of the cardigan were made of the same lace as the skirt, and the tank had some lace on it as well. This was my most successful outfit in white or black. Women wore this outfit to special events. I had to hire a seamstress to sew the skirts. I extended the idea further and made suede and leather skirts with suede and or leather trim on the sweater. These outfits were quite expensive. I could not believe that I had created this!

I expanded my business and sold to boutiques throughout the United States, boutiques in North Miami (Aventura), Las Vegas, and Los Angeles and others. My sales rep would rent a booth at the Kravis Center when there was a fashion fair. That's how we got orders from buyers who lived elsewhere. Someone from Paris wanted to give us an order. That was too difficult; I refused. I was told that Elizabeth Taylor bought one of my sweaters, and that made me very happy.

I learned a great deal about being in business. When you are a teacher, you are living in an ivory tower. You are not in touch with the outside world. You deal with children all day. I knew very little about business in general.

One day, I received a call from a woman who lived in New Jersey. She was opening a boutique store and heard about my sweaters. She asked if she could see them, and she wanted to order a few. She drove from New Jersey to my home in New York. She loved the sweaters but was not ready to place an order now. She would contact me in a few weeks. After she left, she sat in her car, which had been parked in front of my house, for twenty minutes writing something. I was totally unaware of what she was doing.

That week, I had received a call from a renowned boutique in Jamaica Estates, New York. My friend Ilene knew the owners and had set this up for me. I asked her to accompany me, and she happily did. I showed the different sweaters to the owners of the boutique, and they seemed very quiet. When I was through, they informed me that they had just given an order to someone with a few of the exact same sweaters. Ilene and I were mortified! How was this possible? The sweaters were not in the stores or public's possession yet! It then dawned on me! That woman from New Jersey must have been copying my sweaters while she sat in her car. I said, "Was the person with the sweaters from New Jersey?" They said yes. Then I proceeded to describe her. They realized what she had done and immediately cancelled the order. They loved my sweaters and gave me a significant order. Having Ilene there made my story more believable to them. They had been friends for a long time!

A year had passed, and the business was flourishing. A local woman called and asked if she can knit some sweaters. She showed me sweaters that she had knitted, and I hired her. She worked for two months and then left. She had given me a funny excuse. A few weeks later, I was shopping in Woodmere and window gazing as well. To my dismay, I saw one of my sweaters in the window of a boutique store. I had never sold anything to this store. I went in and asked to see that sweater and determined that the quality was not as good as my sweaters, but the pattern and style were mine. I asked who the manufacturer was, and they refused to divulge that information.

Of course, I knew that it was that local woman, but there was no way to prove it. This is very common in the fashion industry. A designer exhibits his or her clothing where each item costs thousands of dollars. A few weeks later, almost the same article of clothing is selling for much, much less.

In 1985, the styles changed completely. Sweaters that were short and body-hugging were now long and humongous. It would cost me twice as much yarn to make a sweater. I would have to pay the knitters twice as much money as well. I hated the new styles, but the world seemed to like them and buy them. I was not getting the orders from stores. They were begging me to make some oversized sweaters, which I refused to do.

Knitting machines were creating beautiful sweaters now. I was asked to become a designer for one of the companies that used knitting machines. The company was in the garment center in Manhattan. I would have to work from 8:00 a.m. to 8:00 p.m. That meant I would have to give up teaching and hardly see my family. I refused to do that! Instead, it was time to close my business and move on to something else. It was a wonderful experience for me and for my family. I was very proud that I was able to create such beautiful clothing and at the same time teach math.

Sailor Sweaters

Ilene & Me

CHAPTER 17

How Did Your Kids and Husband React to Your Life?

My husband, Bob, owned a liquor store in Wall Street. The store was doing quite well, especially during Christmas. They were so busy that he had to sleep at a hotel near the store all week. He would come home on Sundays. They worked late filling orders and delivering them. It was the first time that we didn't feel poor. We were able to go out with friends and even travel. That changed completely when the World Trade Center opened. (Those were the two buildings that were destroyed in 9/11.) Many of his clients moved to the World Trade Center. The liquor store lost half of its clients and more than half of its income. Bob and his partner decided to sell the store. They did not get much for it. The new owners made a poor investment. They had to close the store after one year.

Bob got a job as a liquor salesman. This was not his forte! As a result, he did not get decent orders from liquor stores or bars. He did not do well, and he was depressed. Our relationship suffered because I was successful as a teacher and in business. I could not devote the time to him that he was accustomed to.

My children, on the other hand, were very proud of my business endeavor. When they were teenagers, I tried to instill in them how important a good education is for their future. We could not help them in business, and no one in the family had any knowledge of the business world. They were told that they must help themselves and get professional jobs. And they did! They have become successful adults, and I am very proud of them.

Richard (Rick) was a good student throughout school. He excelled in math, played the clarinet in band, and was on the tennis team. He attended Hebrew school in the afternoon at Temple Hillel and had a bar mitzvah ceremony there and a celebration afterward. After he graduated from Hewlett High School, he attended and graduated from Boston University. He worked as a busboy and waiter during the summer in the Catskills to help support himself. He wanted to be a dentist like his grandfather Irving (Bob's father), but he did not like the sight of blood. He decided to apply to podiatry school. I knew nothing about podiatry. We had never been to a podiatrist. He was admitted at Ohio College of Podiatric Medicine in Cleveland, Ohio; and after four years, he graduated. He did his postgraduate training in St. Louis, Missouri, specializing in foot surgery. He therefore was more certified in the American Board of Podiatric Surgery. We were very proud of him.

One little story! A tennis tournament was being held at North Woodmere Park on Saturday at 4:00 p.m. Bob decided to enter the tournament with Rick as his partner. When the tournament started, Rick had just been awakened from a nap, and he was very lethargic when they were playing. Bob was constantly telling our son as to how poorly he was playing and not moving to hit the ball. At 5:00 p.m., a band arrived at the park and started to practice their music for that night's performance. Suddenly, Rick was energized and started to play tennis, competitively. He was almost dancing to the music. However, the band was playing very loudly, and Bob was getting a headache. While Rick was winning points, Bob started playing poorly. Perhaps young people need loud music to win a tournament, and older people need quiet.

Carol was a fine student and was placed in many enriched classes. She performed in some plays that the schools sponsored, and she also joined the chorus. She studied with the rabbi in a confirmation class. We made her a sweet sixteen party at a local restaurant. She worked as a salesgirl and a waitress in the afternoon and on weekends. She graduated from Hewlett High School a year earlier than her classmates. She got her bachelor's degree at the University of Maryland. She went on to get her master's and doctorate degrees in social work at New York University. She was quite ambitious. Very few people in her field had a doctorate in social work! We were amazed that she had accomplished so much.

Another little story. Carol was about twelve years old, and occasionally, I would make her a cute shirt (blouse). I bought two different floral print fabrics and made her very pretty shirts with puffed sleeves—similar to the puffed sleeve shirts today. She wore one shirt to school, and her friends exclaimed as to how beautiful it was. Then she wore another. Well, they loved that one even more. They asked her where she bought the shirts. She was too embarrassed to say that her mother made them. Instead, she said that we bought them at Abraham and Straus (A&S), which was a half hour from where we lived. One of her friends begged her mother to take her to A&S to buy that shirt. The next day, she confronted Carol and said, "We looked all over A&S and could not find the shirt you wore. We even described it to the saleslady who did not remember it." Carol answered, "I bought them a few weeks ago. They must have sold out!" I laughed when she told me this story. It reminded me of my childhood when I had to wear those fancy dresses that my mother made me! In recent years, she tends to boast about an item that I recently made her. She says, "My mother made it," and she is proud of it!

Bruce was a very good student with little effort. He also played the clarinet in the band and was involved with the tennis team. He had a good sense of humor, would tape us, and imitate us. We all laughed from his antics. He went to Hebrew school and had a bar mitzvah ceremony, and we had a huge celebration at a local temple. Bruce loved magic tricks. He spent all his savings on magic. He would insist that I watch him do the trick and try to figure out how it works. I did most of the time. He then decided to entertain at children's birthday parties with his magic tricks. Of course, they paid him. He worked as a busboy, waiter, and chair boy at Atlantic Beach during the summer. After he graduated from Hewlett High School, he went to Albany University for his bachelor's degree. During his years in college, he started an investment club that was quite successful. He then went to Fordham University for his MBA.

A third little story. Bruce was four and a half, and he was going to start kindergarten the next day for the first time. We had just returned from the beach, and we were emptying the car. We could not find Bruce. We called his name and looked all over. Suddenly, Bruce appeared from the back of the house. I was in complete shock. He had a pair of scissors in his hand, and there was a large bald spot right in front of his head. I said, with tears in my eyes, "Why did you do this?" His response was, "I don't know." I said, "You are starting school tomorrow. What will the kids and teacher think?" Well, the kindergarten teacher thought that he was the cutest with that bald spot. When we told her that he had cut his own hair, she just laughed and laughed!

We had two crazy dogs that Bob and the kids loved. Rusty was a Shetland sheepdog who never barked. The vet told us to have a stranger knock on the windows around the house and make a lot of noise. I asked my brother to do this. We added to the noise as if we were being attacked. We all ran to the front door. Rusty ran there too, did not bark, but made all over the white tile floor!

Our second dog, Chuckles, was a cocker spaniel; and he was very possessive! He loved Carol! One day, Rick was walking up the steps, talking to Carol as he climbed the steps. Chuckles ran to the top of the steps, and he jumped at Rick and bit him on his chest. I wanted to get rid of Chuckles. The tears and expressions of love for the dog were unbelievable! They won! The dog remained!

One night, I was lying in bed watching TV with Chuckles next to me. Bob came into the room to go to the other side of the bed. Chuckles jumped up, ran to the foot of the bed, and started to pace and growl at Bob. He would not let Bob get into that bed. I thought that he was protecting me, so I got out of bed. When I tried to get back into bed, he growled at me as well. This went on for a while, and we didn't know what to do. What would you have done if this happened to you?

My Family

CHAPTER 18

What Other Tennis Clubs Did You Join at That Time?

Atlantic Beach Tennis had become too expensive. Because of this, we decided to look elsewhere. Bob, Ilene, Hal, and I found the Harbor Point tennis club in Freeport that had a pool, a restaurant, and indoor and outdoor tennis courts and was less expensive. We met some lovely people there. After a few years, a builder bought the club and closed it. He built condominiums there. We now had to find another tennis club. Our friend, Dallas, belonged to the Lawrence Tennis Club, but it was very hard to become a member. It was full to capacity! Dallas contacted her friend who had a connection at the Lawrence club. Ilene and I were able to join the ladies' tennis club. It's the old story, "It's whom you know, not what you know." It was a beautiful club with a lovely restaurant and golf course, which required additional membership and fees, of course. We were elated!

We became better tennis players and were included in many tennis games. We entered some tournaments at our level and won a few. We also joined the tennis team and traveled around Long Island to different clubs. It was very interesting to see what these clubs were like. My sister-in-law, Helen, decided to join the Lawrence tennis club as well. We often played tennis together.

After a few years, I was elected president of the ladies' tennis club. This had always been a very active club. Fortunately, Helen was vice president of events. We had a ladies' fashion show using antique clothing from 1950s and '60s. It was a riot! We went to the Hamptons to tour the homes of famous artists. We had a Las Vegas night where we decorated the restaurant to look like a nightclub. Then to everyone's surprise, we hired a handsome young male dancer to entertain us! We worked hard to accomplish this. Two ladies decided to walk out. Helen asked them why. They thought it was inappropriate. So Helen said, "Why don't you run these events next year?" The two ladies said, "Oh, we can't do it!" Then why criticize those who work so hard to entertain you!

I decided to take some golf lessons with the pro at the Lawrence golf course. Much to my surprise, he thought I had potential. I played golf with a few friends and found that I liked tennis much better. To reinforce my thinking, I injured my wrist playing golf. Of course, it was an accident! I could barely hit the tennis ball. That was the end of golf for me.

Me, Dallas & Ilene

Me & Helen

CHAPTER 19

How Did You Start Your Investment Club?

What Were Some of the Things Your Club Did?

When we were at the Harbor Point tennis club, we met several couples who played tennis. We formed a tennis social on Friday night. We would rent four indoor courts. We were eight couples, and the best part was we did not play with our spouses. Somehow, someone else's husband is much sweeter to you when you make an error. We would then go to the local diner for a snack. We did this for several years. Then due to medical reasons, some were no longer able to play tennis. Eventually, we cancelled Friday night tennis.

After all these years together, the ladies decided to form an investment club. This will force us to continue to have contact with each other. We met at someone's house, and we talked about having a meeting once a month at different homes. We were responsible for an initial $500 fee and then $100 each month. They voted for me as president and someone else as treasurer. Three other women were interested in joining the club. It was 1992, and we had eleven ladies in all.

We knew very little about the stock market. I hardly knew anything! I spent time watching CNBC, reading about stocks, and talking to people who were invested in the market. When we accumulated some money, we decided to invest in stocks that were owned by the companies that we were familiar with. We bought Costco, Apple, T.J.Maxx, etc. After a few years, we did very well.

In 1997, we decided to treat our husbands and ourselves to a trip to France. Seven couples went as friends, and surprisingly, they came back as friends. We spent five days in Paris and five days in Nice, the southern part of France, called the "French Riviera." We visited and toured places of interest. We even went to a flea market in Italy. We had lots of fun, and everyone got along so well. As the years went by, we also went to the Nevele Hotel in the Catskills for several weekends.

At times, the ladies would go to Atlantic City for one night and play blackjack, play the slot machines, and shoot craps. Ilene and I would chip in money, to shoot craps. We would consult with each other for each bet. We always lost when we played blackjack, and for some reason, we always won when we played craps. One time, we were at Showboat, and they gave us rooms with air conditioners that were not working. It was now midnight! We were in our nightclothes ready to go to sleep, but we were sweating profusely and could not sleep. We had complained to management but to no avail. We finally received a call telling us to pack our things. They were moving us to new rooms. We had to follow this young man. He took us down to the lobby and over to the next building. Picture this; we were a group of women with no makeup on, in our PJs, traipsing through the lobby with our luggage. We were embarrassed, but when he took us to the penthouse apartment, we forgave all. It was gorgeous, huge, with a beautiful view of the ocean.

There were years when our portfolio increased tremendously. We then gave $5,000 up to $10,000 to each member. We still have an investment club, but only six members remain. It has really been a wonderful, educational, and social experience. Investing in the stock market has helped me greatly with my personal finances as well.

CHAPTER 20

When Did Love, Marriage, and Family Happen?

I am sure my family has been waiting for this chapter!

Coincidentally, I went to the same beauty salon as Alisa's mother. It was during the summer, and Alisa was hired to substitute for the receptionist, who went on vacation. Rick needed a haircut, and I recommended that he use my hairdresser, who also cuts men's hair. He met Alisa casually. During their conversation, Rick realized that he knew her brother Larry from BU, and the following weekend, he went to AJ's, a restaurant and bar in Atlantic Beach. Alisa was there with a friend. She was wearing a lovely dress and makeup. It may not have been love at first sight, but he called her the next morning for a date that day. They started to date, and within a short period of time, it became quite serious. Alisa was getting her master's degree at Washington University in St. Louis. When Rick completed Podiatry School, he managed to get an internship in St. Louis where Alisa was. He proposed, she accepted, and they got engaged in 1981.

They came back to New York and made plans for our families to meet. We were vacationing in Florida, visiting my father who lived in Hallandale. We met Barbara and Murray, Alisa's parents, and her grandmother, whom Alisa adored, at Boca Lago in Florida. Their primary home was in North Woodmere, New York, where we also lived. We talked about a wedding in May. Murray said that they will take care of everything. He was a very generous guy! They had a beautiful wedding at Temple Israel in May 1982. They rented an apartment in Howard Beach, New York; had Ryen in November '83; bought a house in Muttontown, New York; and then had Brett in '86.

Rick opened a podiatry office in Bellerose, New York. Then a few years later, he opened a second office, with a partner, in Huntington, New York. About ten years after, Rick, his partner, and his accountant bought an eyeglass store in Manhattan, New York. This store serviced two unions, with an enrollment of thousands of people. It was and still is a great investment!

Alisa was now a certified social worker, and her practice dealt with families and young children. She had her own office but eventually shared an office with Rick. She worked part time. Rick would make dinner, help with homework, etc., when she worked. She loved the fact that our family played tennis. She decided to learn how to play tennis. She took a lot of tennis lessons and became an excellent player. She would invite me to her club to be her partner in a tournament, and we would win. I was a weaker player, but I must have risen to the occasion. I invited her to my club as well, and once again, we would win. Alisa and Rick recently started playing golf, and they are doing very well. Her greatest strength is making all the holiday dinners. She does all the cooking with some help from Rick. One year, she had twenty-six guests at a sit-down Passover dinner!

Bob and I would go every weekend to see Ryen and Brett. We would watch them play softball and soccer. When they were older, we went to their concerts where they played in the band. We were always invited to any event that involved the children. Although Ryen was a fine student, there were times that he would call me for help with a difficult math problem. I loved helping him just on the phone. We did not have FaceTime then. I was pleased with myself that I remembered how to solve the problem. After high school, Ryen went to Boston University. In his senior year, Ryen went to a popular bar where he met Dana whom he knew for many years. With her was her friend Shari. Shari was a senior at BU as well. At the end of the evening, Ryen drove Shari back to BU. They exchanged phone numbers, and Ryen called Shari for a date. She "blew him off"! He then invited her to a concert. She accepted, and that was the beginning of a love affair.

After they graduated from BU in 2005, Ryen got a job with Segal Advisors. He is currently senior vice president. Shari is a school psychologist in Queens, New York. They dated for six years, finally got married, and had a beautiful country club wedding in 2011. Two years later, Shari gave birth to twin girls, Avery and Leah. They bought a lovely house in Roslyn Heights, New York. That made me a great-grandmother, and I love being with them. They are so beautiful, talented, and creative. I feel as though some of my creative genes have gone to them. Of course, they have gone to my children and grandchildren as well!

When they were six years old, the family visited with me. Avery and Leah asked me to show them everything that I made. They were so inquisitive! We walked around the house, and I pointed to my sculptures and paintings and crafts. I tried to teach them how to crochet a chain stitch, but they were too young. They are nine now and can crochet. Ryen and I entered a family tennis tournament on the highest level at Boca West. Surprisingly, we won but not due to me. He is an excellent tennis player and enjoys winning and sending me videos of his matches.

Someone was smart enough to introduce Jamie and Brett. They dated for several weeks when Brett realized that the family would be going to Aruba for one week around Christmastime. Brett asked his parents if he could bring Jamie. They said yes! Obviously, Brett was very attracted to Jamie and she to him. When he asked Jamie to go to Aruba, she did consult with her parents, and the response was *yes*! That week cemented their relationship! They went back to Aruba the following year. Brett presented Jamie with a beautiful engagement ring and proposed marriage. Jamie's parents, Jill and Larry, met Brett's parents at a restaurant in New York. Once again, a wedding was planned. It occurred at the Hilton Hotel in Westchester, New York, in May 2017. It was a weekend affair, and we celebrated all weekend.

Brett was a different kind of student. He was very smart and was able to build computers from scratch. He was very knowledgeable with computers when most kids knew little or nothing. While he was in high school, he had a part-time job at a bank and received a promotion because of his computer ability. They even offered to pay all college expenses if he agreed to work for the bank when he graduated. He refused. He went to Rollins College near Orlando, Florida, and graduated in 2008.

Brett was looking for a job in the Boca Delray area. At the same time, he was looking for a place to live. I offered him the upstairs part of my house. He lived there for about four months, and it was a pleasure to have him around. He was so grateful that he would barbeque dinner for us. Through a friend from college, he was able to obtain a job at Mr. Cooper in Coral Gables, Florida. He is now the assistant vice president at this mortgage company. He moved to Coral Gables and then to Miami. He asked me to go shopping with him to pick out furniture for his apartment. He had no idea as to what to buy. I helped him decorate his apartment, and when Shari and Ryen bought a house, I helped them as well. Jamie completed her doctorate in psychology at Miami University and did a postdoctoral program also. She helped publish some books on their research in child psychology. She also started a private practice, became pregnant, and gave birth to Ethan in October 2019. They bought a beautiful large house in Boca Raton. Two and a half years later, she gave birth to Eliana in April 2022. Ethan reminds me of Brett and Rick (his grandfather). He is constantly opening and closing doors, gates, etc. He loves cars and pushing buttons. Eliana is a quiet, adorable baby so far. It's wonderful that they live in Boca Raton. I often make matzo ball soup for us and them, especially when someone doesn't feel well. It's considered "Jewish Penicillin."

Alisa, Rick & Their Family

Carol loved to swim at the New York University gym where she was going for her master's. She spotted this cute guy running around the track. He spotted her as well. She thought that he was Spanish, and he thought that she was Italian. She met Deivy and learned that he was from São Paulo, Brazil. His parents fled from the Holocaust, tried to get into the United States and couldn't, and settled in Brazil. There are over one hundred thousand Jews living in São Paulo. Deivy was getting his doctorate in mathematics at NYU. Carol was now working at New York Hospital. Deivy encouraged Carol to go for a doctorate in social work, and she did.

They were now dating for one year. The family met Deivy, and I thought that he was very nice. We had a lot in common because I taught math, and he also intended to teach math. It was the beginning of November 1988, and I picked Carol up at the Long Island railroad. As soon as she saw me, she said, "We want to get married within the next few months, and we want a small wedding in NYC (Manhattan)." This was almost an impossibility! How can we make arrangements for invitations, a Rabbi and ceremony, a wedding gown for her and a gown for me, and a place to have the celebration in such a short time? Well, they were married on February 4, 1989, at the Spanish and Portuguese Temple on Central Park West; and everything was accomplished! Deivy's parents (Chansel and Jonel) and sister Marella traveled from Brazil to New York for the wedding. We had lots of fun!

They lived on Fifth Avenue and 15th Street. By 1992, Carol and Deivy were both completing their doctorates when Carol became pregnant. She was at the end of her ninth month when she had to "defend her doctorate" before a group of professors. Thank goodness, she was successful because the next day, she gave birth to Ilana. It was June 18, 1993. A few weeks later, Deivy had to go through a similar experience to defend his doctorate. Deivy got a math teaching position at the University of Recife—a northeastern city in Brazil. They packed, took what they could, and left for Recife when Ilana was about seven weeks old. We were upset but could not change the situation. There are difficult times when we have no control, but we must live with it and do the best we can. Bob and I decided that we would travel to Brazil as much as we are able to.

Carol and Deivy rented an apartment in Recife in a very nice area. The street that borders the Atlantic Ocean in Recife is beautiful. There are hotels and spacious homes similar to A1A in Palm Beach. However, once you go more than two blocks from the ocean, there's a lot of poverty. The apartments that you rent have just walls and some cabinets in the kitchen. You must rent or buy clothing closets, stoves, refrigerators, washers, and furniture. There is only hot water when you take a shower. You must boil water to wash dishes and pots. You cannot have a clothes dryer because the electricity is not strong enough. After you wash clothes, towels, and sheets, they must be hung on a clothesline in the apartment to dry. When they are dry, they are stiff as a board; and you must iron everything, including socks and underwear. It was very difficult for Carol! She had to take care of an infant and all the chores. She spoke very little Portuguese, and no one spoke English. If you have traveled, you are under the impression that everyone speaks English. Not true! People who work in hotels or take you on tours speak English. However, if you live in a foreign country and go to the market, they only speak their language. She was able to hire a woman for only $5 per day who performed all the chores in the apartment. That was the going rate, and it was very helpful.

Bob and I were finally able to travel to Recife. The apartment was nice, and Ilana was an adorable baby, who was now four months old. Carol heard of an island that is interesting to visit. We had to take a bus. All the passengers stared at us as if we were from another planet. Ilana had blonde hair and blue eyes, and I don't think they ever saw that before. We ate lunch at a stand. Finally, a small boat anchored near us. We had to remove our shoes and walk in the water, and someone helped us onto the boat. The boat sailed across the lake to an island. Once again, we had to walk in the water to the shore. I could not believe that people would recommend that we see this island. There was a food stand, a bathroom and a few chairs, lounges, and umbrellas that were so thin that the sun came right through. We were getting sunburned, and Ilana was very red. We decided to leave, had to wait for the boat, and finally got to the other side. We needed a bathroom. We walked a bit and were astounded to see a huge pool and a beautiful hotel in this underdeveloped area. We jumped into the pool, and it sizzled from our hot bodies! The manager of the hotel was very kind and allowed us to use the facilities.

After one year, Deivy received a teaching position at the University of São Paulo where his family lived. They were overjoyed! We visited them twice a year, and Carol would come to New York with Ilana once a year. We twice extended the trip to include Buenos Aires, and with Helen and Morty, we went to Rio de Janeiro. São Paulo was an interesting experience. If you have eaten at a Brazilian restaurant here, you then know how delicious the food is. Deivy's father, Jonel, took us to a renowned restaurant. I particularly loved the cheese rolls. Deivy said, "They are so easy to make. I will get you the flour that you have to use tomorrow." We had an afternoon flight back to New York. Just before we left, Deivy came back with four bags of white flour in clear plastic bags. It looked like cocaine was in those bags. I refused to take them. He insisted and slipped them into my extra bag that I was carrying. I was so nervous going through security. I was sure that they would detain me and question me, and I would miss my flight back to New York. Fortunately, I passed through security easily.

In 1996, she gave birth to Alexandre (Alex); and three months later, they returned to the United States and settled in Florida. Deivy taught at one of the universities, and Carol started a practice there. They lived near Grandma Mabel (Bob's mother) and then bought a house in Hollywood. After five years in Florida, they decided to move up north and eventually bought a house in Media, Pennsylvania. Deivy taught math at one of the universities; and Carol opened a practice, first in Wilmington, Delaware, and another in Media, Pennsylvania. Bob and I would travel to Media on special occasions, such as birthdays, holidays, and school events. We would stay for the weekend. They were wonderful hosts, and Deivy would cook special dishes for us that were delicious.

Ilana did very well in school. She also studied at a nearby temple. She was bas mitzvah and had a beautiful celebration. She was in the chorus and the band. When she went to high school, she auditioned for the school play. She was only a freshman; however, she has a beautiful voice, and she received the part that she auditioned for. She continued to get major roles in school productions throughout high school. By the time she was a junior, she had a group of people who followed her performances. They said that she "lit up the stage." I thought so also! When she graduated, I said to Ilana, "Maybe you should audition for a role in a play in college." She said, "I would get so nervous when I have to do my part. I am so happy that I don't have to do that anymore!" I had no idea!

When Ilana was little, she always drew pictures with a magic marker or charcoal. She loved art but did not pursue it. She received her bachelor's and Master's Degrees in forensic psychology. She worked for a hedge fund but felt this was not for her. She went back to her first love, which was art. She has exhibited her art in many galleries in Manhattan and Brooklyn and at the Art Basil Show in Miami. She is currently the cofounder of an art organization. On her paintings and in person, she is now referred to as LaLa! The family, however, likes to call her "Mini Mimi."

Alex started to play tennis when he was young. He would force his mother to play with him. He went to tennis camps in the summertime and got much better. We often played together, Alex against Carol and me. Alex and I recently played in a family match at Boca West and won, due to him, of course. He loved Federer! He watched all his matches, and he made his mother buy him Federer's line of clothing.

He went to a nearby temple, was bar mitzvah there, and had a celebration afterward. I crocheted sixty yarmulkes for the males and sixty lace hankies to be worn by the females. I had done the same for Ilana and all my male children and grandchildren. He played on the tennis team in high school. He learned how to fence and participated in many tournaments and won some. After he graduated from high school, he applied at the University of Pennsylvania. He was accepted. We were all thrilled! After he graduated, he worked for a commercial real estate company for several years. He then decided to go for his MBA. Fortunately, he got into Wharton and is now completing his second year. He has received a few letters of praise from some of his professors. He had an internship in London this summer at a very prestigious financial company.

He called me recently and said, "Grandma, I tell my friends about you, your age, and your childhood stories. They love to hear about these stories, and they ask for more and more. You should write a book about your life." Alex put that thought into my brain, and I could not stop thinking about it. So this is the result of that conversation.

Carol, Deivy & Their Family

Bruce rented at Fire Island, Long Island, New York, for the summer months. He went there on weekends and managed the house that he lived in. Many young adults rented at Fire Island. The beaches were beautiful, concerts were available, and there were parties galore! Lori was a manager of another house, not too far from where Bruce lived. Lori attended a party, which took place in the house that Bruce managed, and they were formally introduced. After that, they met again, coincidentally, at a local bar in Fire Island and just talked. They dated in New York City twice, but they were just friends. One day, Lori's sister Sharon was visiting, and they went to the beach. Sharon saw Bruce there and, pointing to Bruce, said to Lori, "He's cute! Why don't you get to know him better?" Lori followed her sister's proposal. They started dating steadily in Fire Island. Bruce was living and working in Manhattan, and Lori worked in New Jersey and lived in Hoboken, New Jersey.

On the way back from Fire Island to New York City, Bruce and Lori stopped at my house. Bruce claims that my first question was, "Is she Jewish?" I don't believe it! Bruce had called earlier to tell me that they were coming, so I invited them for dinner. I had leftovers in the freezer. Lori loved the chicken and mushrooms that I served and makes that same recipe today. They were engaged in 1992. We met Saul (Lori's dad) at a restaurant in New Jersey and planned a wedding. They had a beautiful wedding in Livingston, New Jersey.

They rented an apartment in New York City on 23rd Street and Second Avenue. Bruce was interviewed and hired by Rabobank in New York City to work in the credit department. At that time, it was a small division of this bank, which has offices around the world. He is now executive director of Value Chain Finance. Lori graduated from Hofstra University in 1987. She then worked for a cosmetic printing firm. She was the senior sales director and the most productive saleslady of the staff. She got orders from famous cosmetic companies that no one else was able to get.

Brandon was born in January 1997. He would not let his parents diaper him when I visited. He cried and kicked and only wanted me to do it. When I tried to diaper him, he lay there like a doll, smiling and happy. He was so cute with me. We could not understand why this was happening. I did the exact same thing that they did. We were never able to figure this out. Lori and Bruce bought a lovely house on a hill in Livingston, New Jersey. Lori's mother was ill and died when Lori was young. She felt responsible for her younger sisters, Sharon and Erica. She wanted to be near her sisters, who were still living at home in Livingston, New Jersey. Shortly thereafter, Jamie was born in July 1999. She was a quiet, beautiful baby. In November 2004, Jessie was born. She was the darling of the family. Lori constantly lectured the children on their behavior. When we went to a restaurant, they fought as to who will sit next to her. Nothing beats love!

Brandon went to Livingston High School, which was a very competitive school, and he did very well. He was on the tennis team and joined the Model UN club. He belonged to several honor societies. After he graduated, he went to George Washington University and majored in finance. He graduated in three and a half years. He worked for two finance firms, and he now works for Citibank in an executive capacity. Brandon was visiting me at Boca West last Christmas (2021) when he met Olivia, whom he knew casually from GW. They dated that night and have continued dating. Brandon lives and works in New York City, and Olivia lives and works in DC. They have managed to do a lot of traveling to be together. When they visited me this spring, we taught them how to play Rummikub. They loved the game, bought two games, and are addicted to playing Rummikub.

Jamie was very busy in Livingston High School. She was president of the Friendship Circle and vice president of Craft for a Cause. She also volunteered at the temple the family went to. After high school, she went to the University of Delaware. She majored in communications and advertising. In the summer, she had various jobs. She was a counselor, worked for a skin care company, and worked in a health juice store. Jamie graduated last year and was immediately hired by a perfume firm. She now works for an international pharmaceutical company that specializes in skin care. I would often visit. I would take the Long Island train to Penn station and transfer to the New Jersey Transit. Bruce would pick me up at South Orange. It was a tough trip. I much preferred driving, but my kids were not happy about me driving. I would come for the weekend on special occasions and leave on Monday morning. Jamie was always busy in her room, and when we had dinner, she did not say much. When I was ready to leave, she would run down the steps, hug me, and say, "I love you so much, Grandma. Don't leave!" I looked at her in amazement and said, "Jamie, we hardly spoke to each other all weekend." She now was surprised! This situation has changed drastically. She was here last Christmas and was so outgoing and lively. I could not believe it was the same Jamie. About a year ago, she met Trey on an online dating app, and they have been dating ever since. They are both quite young but very serious about each other. We shall see what the future brings!

Jessie was always an independent child. Brandon and Jamie wanted to smother her with hugs and kisses. She seldom allowed it. She loved playing soccer and was very good at it. She would make a lot of goals, and she was invited into the traveling soccer team . . . which was an honor. At Livingston High School, she is in mostly honor or AP classes. She is a senior and is in the process of interviewing at the colleges of her choice. Jessie had to write about the American dream for her English class last semester. She decided to interview me because I represented the American dream to her. She asked me numerous questions about my childhood and family. She received an A for the essay from her teacher. When I read it, I was very touched by what she had written and how it was presented. She sent me an e-mail of the essay, and I in turn, sent it to all my children and grandchildren. This article also helped create this memoir.

Brandon, Jamie, and Jessie had lovely bar and bas mitzvah ceremonies at their temple; and we celebrated with beautiful catered affairs afterward.

Lori, Bruce & Their Family

CHAPTER 21

How Was Your Life After You Retired?

In 1992, I was given a very difficult class to teach. They were below grade level in most of their subjects, and there were a few boys who had behavior problems. In the past, when I taught these "general" classes, I was able to improve their ability and interest by teaching them some algebra. Their self-image improved, and some went on to average classes. Parents would thank me for getting their children into average classes.

I tried to consult with the vice principal and principal. They were unable to get these boy's parents to cooperate. They told me that I must handle it myself. One day, I had to raise my voice to get their attention. Well, my heart started to palpitate, and I thought I was having a heart attack. I did not feel well. I was weak and had to sit down. The next day, I broke out in a rash all over my body. I did not feel that I would last through the end of the school year. After consulting with my husband about our finances, I decided to retire. I would get social security and a pension, and we would be able to manage. My husband retired as well.

I knew that I had to be active and find other interests. I enrolled in several adult education classes. I took a class in finance, but it was not what I thought it would be. I took several classes in bridge and did play it for a while. When I learned to play canasta, I found it more enjoyable and gave up bridge.

I also registered for a class in sculpture, which became the best art course I had ever taken. I had taken painting classes and craft classes previously, but I liked sculpture better. I continued to take sculpture for many years. I started with clay and went on to use alabaster, papier-mâché, a hard foam used on decks, travertine, and marble—which is the hardest surface of all. I started with a hammer and chisel and went to all kinds of electric tools, which was very difficult. When I went to Florida, I took sculpture classes at the Boca Raton Museum and had two of my sculptures exhibited there. At Boca West, I conducted a lecture about sculpture for the Special Interest Group and displayed some of my pieces. At another time, I offered to allow members to come to my home to see all my sculptures. I have them on display all over my house.

Now that we were retired, we traveled in the United States and abroad. We finally decided to spend the winters in Florida. We first rented at Boca West for three months because our friends were there. However, we could not use the facilities unless we paid an exorbitant amount of money to join the club for only three months. We then rented at Hunters Run in Boynton Beach where they allowed us all the privileges the owners had for a small fee. I joined the tennis team and enjoyed playing with ladies from other places. After two years, you had to buy or leave Hunters Run. We chose to leave, primarily because it was too far from our friends in Boca and much too far from Hallandale where my daughter and family were now living. We bought at Boca Lago, and once again, I joined the tennis team. Three years later, our circumstances changed, and we were able to buy at Boca West.

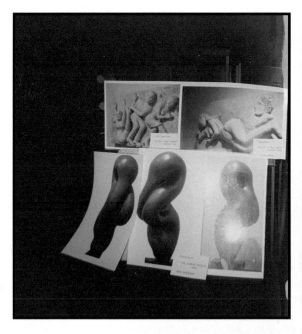

My Sculptures

CHAPTER 22

What Happened to Your Husband, Bob?

It was May 2000; we had just returned home from visiting Lori, Bruce, and the kids. The house was hot and muggy. Bob turned the thermostat down and put on the air conditioner in the dining room. The AC did not come on. He went to the other thermostat in the family room, and again, nothing happened! He kept running up and down the steps in great frustration, yelling and sweating. He finally called the AC company, and they could not send someone until the next morning! It was ninety-five degrees in the house, and we finally fell asleep after midnight.

At four in the morning, I was awakened from a terrible sound uttered by Bob. He was in a coma! I called 911, and they were here in a few minutes. They rushed him to the hospital. He had a bleeding stroke, and he was scheduled for brain surgery that morning. He was in a coma on a respirator for several days after the surgery and was unable to speak or walk and did not understand when we spoke to him. He was in the hospital for one month and then in rehab for another month. When he came home, he walked with a cane; but in a week, he was able to walk independently. However, he was only able to say two words at a time. He had aphasia, which means he could not retrieve words. He could not read or write or understand anything. It was very sad for the whole family. I was his only caregiver, and it was very sad for me. We sold the spit-level house we lived in and bought a basically one-level house.

On October 2000, his mother Mabel died, and he inherited some money. We traveled to Florida and bought a house near the tennis facility so that Bob could walk to the tennis courts. We moved in on December 15 that year. Bob took tennis lessons and started playing with men at the lowest level. This made him very happy. After four years, he was able to say a simple sentence.

Lori, Bruce, and the kids were visiting us, eating breakfast in the kitchen, when Bob walked in. He said to them, "I'm so glad that you were able to come here." He then fell to the ground and went into a coma. Bruce and I were in a state of shock! We could not move! Lori called 911. They took him to the hospital. We were told that there was nothing that they could do for him. He would be a "vegetable"! He died in January 2004.

I could not live in that new house. There were too many bitter memories. Once again, I had to sell a house, and I did and moved into a community called Meadowbrook Pointe. It provided you with a clubhouse and tennis courts in Westbury, New York. My lifestyle was six months in New York and six months in Boca. Last year, I decided to sell my apartment in New York and become a year-round resident of Florida. It was a good decision and certainly a less stressful way of life!

My Husband Bob

CHAPTER 23

How Did Playing Tennis Affect Your Life?

Playing tennis has helped make me what I am today. It has affected me physically, mentally, and socially. The movements provided by playing tennis is enough exercise for me. This has kept me in good form physically. While playing, I expand my mind mentally, thinking about where to hit the ball, how to make a good shot, the score, and what I did wrong. We meet before we play and interact with people, and every time we change sides during play, we rest and socialize. When Chrissie Evert came to Boca West as a guest speaker and said that she was old at age sixty-two, I raised my hand and referred to the above items and how it has helped bring me to this tender age in relatively good health. So keep playing tennis! Fortunately, I am still playing tennis with people who are young enough to be my children or grandchildren. For many years, I never disclosed my age. I was afraid that if I had a bad tennis day (which happens to all of us), the ladies would say, "Who wants to play with that old lady?" But it's funny; they all tell me that they want to be like me when they reach my age. They seem to know my age!

For many years, I played tennis with my friend Ilene and occasionally with Dallas. Ilene and I joined the tennis team for seniors. It was a newly formed team, and Merry was the captain. She asked us to co-captain it with her. We did that for one season. It was fun visiting all the other clubs, playing tennis, and winning when possible.

Several years ago, I met another Mimi L. at Boca West tennis. I was called Mimi with a short "I." And she was from Canada, and they called her Mimi with a long "I." We decided to play together. We were partners, and we did remarkably well. We seemed to complement each other. We decided to enter tournaments together and even went to Member/Guest as a couple. It was surprising to us that we were able to win at these events. She would rally, and I would put the ball away from our opponents. It was a good combination. We started to socialize with our boyfriends, and we became very good friends. We are in touch with each other throughout the entire year.

Now for a few tennis stories!

Andi and I were playing for the Boca West team, and we won the first set. We were in the second set, and the score was 5–4. and I was serving at 40–30. I served the ball, and the opposing team's lady could not return it. This meant that we won the game and won the set and won the match. We jumped for joy! The opposing lady suddenly said that the serve was out. We felt that the call was late and not true. It was her call, and there was nothing that we could do about it. We were very upset and could barely hit the ball. They won that game and the next two games and won that set. We now went into a ten-point tiebreaker instead of a third set. The score in the tiebreaker was now 5–7 in their favor. We were changing sides. Our team was watching us play, and they told us, "You have to forget what happened and concentrate on playing." I said, "I know what can help me." I retrieved a packet of gum from my bag. I insisted that Andi chew the gum as well as me because it will relax us. We chewed that gum, won the tiebreaker, and won the match, all due to chewing gum!

When I lived at Boca Lago, I also played on the tennis team. There were two ladies who thought that they were better than the rest of us. I now lived in Boca West, and we had to play against Boca Lago. Dorothy and I had to play against these two "uppity" ladies. Dorothy was very nervous and was not playing well. They had won the first set, and the score was 1–5 in their favor in the second set when it started to rain. We made plans to finish the match on the following Monday at Boca Lago. They only needed to win one more game to win. My partner did not want to bother to play. She wanted to forfeit the match. I said, "Let's play. We have to for the team." She finally agreed. I also told her that she was a much better player than they were. We started winning games and miraculously won the second set. They were devastated and started playing poorly. We went into a ten-point tiebreaker and won it. "Never give up the ship!" Your mental attitude helps determine how you play. A positive attitude is always helpful!

Bob and our grandson Ryen—who was sixteen years old—entered a tournament. They won the first set. In the second set, Bob ran to hit the ball and pulled his hamstring in his leg. He was in a lot of pain but refused to stop playing. He was determined to win under any circumstances. He told Ryen, "You run for the ball as if you are playing singles, and I'll hit whatever I can." Believe it or not, they won the match! Bob's hamstring took six months to heal completely.

Mimi L. & Me

Alisa & Me

CHAPTER 24

Have You Ever Met Famous People?

Elvis Presley

We were in Las Vegas, and we had tickets to see Elvis. I was about forty-four years old and in my prime! I wore a tight white sweater and more makeup than I usually wear. I only wore moisturizer and lipstick then. We got to the door of the event, and Bob tipped the maître d'. The maître d' brought a small table and two chairs to the center area of the stage and told us to sit there. We were absolutely delighted! Elvis sang a few of his songs, and he stared at me while he was singing I stared back. Of course, I was thrilled! His practice was to hand out white silk handkerchiefs to the ladies. He handed me a handkerchief first; and four ladies, who were sitting behind me, grabbed it right out of my hands. Elvis witnessed the whole thing. He took another handkerchief, rolled it up, walked over to where I was sitting, and placed it in my hand. I thanked him, and this time, I was really thrilled!

The following week, I was back teaching a class when a boy raised his hand to ask me a question. I thought it was about something that he did not understand in reference to what I was teaching. He said, "Mrs. Sherman, were you in Las Vegas last week, and were you at an Elvis show? I saw you on TV at an Elvis show." I had no idea that they were taping that show. "That's my claim to fame!"

Michael Douglas

Every year, Merry made herself a mystery birthday trip. This particular year, she took thirty women to New York, and I was one of them. For lunch, we went to the Boathouse in Central Park. The ladies said, "Did you see him? Did you see him?" I asked who. They said, "Michael Douglas." I finished lunch and went to the ladies' room. Once again, the ladies were talking excitedly about Michael Douglas. I asked, "Where is he sitting?" They said, "When you leave the bathroom, look to your left." I walked out, looked to my left, and something propelled me to run over to Michael Douglas. He was there with a woman with long brown hair. I did not see her face. Sitting between them was the cutest boy, who was about three years old. I exclaimed, "Michael Douglas, I love you in all your movies, and this little boy is a clone of you." He stood up and thanked me. He looked much younger than he appeared on screen, much thinner and shorter than I had imagined that he would be.

Suddenly, the woman turned her head; and I realized that it was his wife, Catherine Zeta-Jones. I said to her, "And you are gorgeous." I then realized what I had done, and I was quite embarrassed. I started to apologize. They said it was OK. I was a little relieved. I wished them a hearty lunch and left. When I got back to my seat and told the ladies what I had done, they could not believe it and thought that I was a little "crazy." I think that they were jealous that they did not have that experience. When I think about it now, I feel as if a force pushed me there, and I had no control over it.

Frank Sinatra

Bob and I and Ilene and Hal went to Westbury Music Fair in New York to see Frank Sinatra. It was his seventy-fifth birthday, and he was performing that evening. His performance was not up to par, but it was exciting just being there and listening to him sing. At the end of the period of intermission, he appeared again, and people were going up to him and speaking to him. Of course, they may have been relatives. I said to Ilene, "Let's go down to the stage and shake his hand and congratulate him for his birthday." We went down to the stage, shook Frank Sinatra's hand, and told him how great he was and that we loved his music. He was very receptive. He went on to sing more of his favorite songs but was beginning to look a little tired. Everyone applauded when the show was over but were disappointed because he did not return to the stage for a curtain call.

CHAPTER 25

What Was Your Experience like with Murray?

In 2006, my husband was gone for two and a half years. I had some dates but no one special. I was visiting in New York and had an evening flight back to Boca. I had nothing to do. It was Monday, and Boca West had a singles event on Monday nights. I changed my flight, got in at 5:00 p.m., changed my clothing, and met my girlfriend at the golf building where the event took place. Murray's cousin, who lived at the Polo Club, asked Murray to sign her in at the singles event. He did that and decided to walk around the room. I was standing at the bar with my friend when he stopped to talk to me. We chatted for a while, and then he asked if I would join him elsewhere for coffee. I agreed, and we continued to see each other for the next eight years. In 2007, after dating for one year, he moved in with me. He told me that the prior year, he was only losing one step, but now he was losing two steps. I did not pay much attention to it. We went on several cruises and many events at Boca West where we ate and danced and had fun.

By 2011, Murray was repeating what he said in the morning several times during the day. He was also asking the same question like, "What time is dinner?" many times. I consulted with his stepdaughter, who was a psychiatrist, and she set up an appointment for him to be evaluated at Columbia Presbyterian Hospital in New York. They determined that he had the beginnings of Alzheimer's disease, and they gave him some medication.

He got progressively worse. He would lose the car. He would get lost going to the bathroom at a restaurant or movie. The police would deliver him home or call me to pick him up. I couldn't leave him alone and hired an aid, but he wouldn't let her into the apartment. I enrolled him in many classes, hoping that it would prevent the disease from getting worse, but to no avail!

In 2015, we were invited for Father's Day to Alisa and Rick's home in New York for a barbeque. When we came home from the barbeque, he began to show signs of becoming violent. This frightened me! As difficult as it was for me to decide, I knew that we could no longer live together. I called his other stepdaughter, who lived in Florida, and told her what was happening. I also told her that we cannot live together anymore, that I am afraid that he may do something violent to me. She had to find an assisted living place for him in Florida. She mentioned that she cannot have him live with her. She found a place in Deerfield Beach. I was able to get him there. But he became aggressive, and he hit me. I visited him several days later, and again, he was aggressive. His stepdaughter called me and told me that I can no longer visit him. That was the last time I saw him!

Me & Murray

CHAPTER 26

How Did You Get Involved with Performing in Shows?

Why Did You Decide to Go on YouTube?

We had just moved into North Woodmere; and I was very busy with Carol, who was seven months old, and Rick, who was three years old. I became friendly with Janet, who asked me to join her one evening. We were going to go to where she had lived to participate in the chorus of "Pajama Game." We were also part of the dance team. I had never performed in anything! I had to learn some songs for the chorus and had to practice the routines for the dancing. I really enjoyed it! Bob was the babysitter, and he agreed to let me rehearse once a week. The show was a success, and the director gave me a speaking part in the next show.

Years later, my temple decided to raise money by selling tickets to a member participation Broadway show. They hired the same director, and the show they selected was *Damn Yankees*. The children were older, and we did not need a babysitter. Bob decided to join the show with me. He was one of the baseball players, and I had a minor part and was one of the dancers and in the chorus. It was fun! The next year, I sang "Do-Re-Mi" from *The Sound of Music*, with eight small children, including my own, at a temple show.

In "the five towns" where I lived, Corinne wrote and directed shows every year. They were individual acts, and they were performed at the local high school. I was asked to audition for one of her shows. I was very nervous and sang, "I love New York in June." Corinne offered me a solo song. I could not believe it! I sang "I'm Just a Girl Who Cain't Say No" in an abbreviated costume. All my friends and family attended the performance. I continued to be in her shows for several years.

After I moved to Boca West, Esther moved here as well. She would write, produce, direct, and accompany the singers on the piano. She would produce a show every year for the special interest club. I became part of the acting group, and I would try to help her with props and costumes. My best part was playing Queen Esther and in the last show before the coronavirus pandemic. I sang one of my favorite songs, "Bei Mir Bistu Shein." We had a lot of fun during rehearsals!

My daughter Carol and my granddaughter, Ilana, insisted that I make a video on You-Tube. They wanted me to talk about the drugstore makeup that I use and to demonstrate how I apply the makeup. Ilana was the photographer, director, and editor. Carol was the props girl and commentator. I had over one thousand viewers. Then they felt that I should make another video about my morning routine, what I have for breakfast, and my general views about diet and staying healthy. After that, Ilana asked me to make a video on simple sewing stitches. I had taught Ilana and Carol how to do a backstitch, a running stitch, and an overcast stitch and how to make a hem. Her friends have been asking her to fix clothing for them because they could not afford a dressmaker. I made that video for her friends and hopefully for other people who have the need to fix their own clothing and not be dependent on a tailor. Go to YouTube, and the name of the channel is "Mimi and Ilana's Health and Beauty Secrets."

MIMI SHERMAN

Performing At Boca West

CHAPTER 27

How Do You Manage to Look So Young?

At the age of 94

My mother-in-law, Mabel, was a very attractive woman. I met her in 1950 when she was forty-four. She wore designer clothes, lots of makeup, false eyelashes and pinky red hair. However, she had huge bags under her eyes. Really huge! When she was fifty years old, she had plastic surgery to remove those bags. It was more than the average eye surgery, and therefore, her recuperation was much longer. She stayed home for four months. She now needed to do something about her developing wrinkled skin. She wanted a face-lift. Her husband, Irving, was totally against it. He felt that she was not a good candidate because it took her so long to heal. He refused to allow her to do it. It would take her five hours to put on makeup, and various creams did not help. She became a "hermit." She did not leave her apartment except to see a doctor. She wore a kerchief to hide her face.

Bob and I witnessed all that happened with her. We both felt that we would never allow this to happen to me. I had always looked younger than I was. When my face lost its youthful appearance, it was time to do something. I did see a doctor and had a procedure. Through the years, I have gone to dermatologists to have injections. I have tried all kinds of creams, constantly looking for the fountain of youth. Recently, I was at the Hard Rock Hotel in Hollywood, Florida; and in a store in the mall, I discovered "LED light therapy." I have had several treatments, and I feel that it has helped me significantly.

There are always other factors that determine your appearance. There's the genetic factor, your diet, the vitamins you consume, and how you spend your day. I eat five small meals rather than two or three large ones. It is not healthy to go to sleep with a full stomach of food. It is also not healthy to starve yourself all day and then make up for it in the evening. Your metabolism should work all day to digest your food and not overwork at night. I am not a sedentary person. I still play tennis, and when I am home watching TV or sewing or knitting and crocheting, I constantly get up. I get a drink of water, stretch my body, and just do something. Sitting for a long period of time is not good for you.

I play sudoku to activate my brain. I also play canasta three times each week. In addition, it gives you an opportunity to socialize. Playing canasta keeps your mind alert. With the blossoming of technology, many of my peers have been intimidated. I have embraced a lot of it. I use an iPhone, a laptop, and recently an Apple Watch. I feel that your attitude and your state of being has a lot to do with your health and the way you look. It is important to me to be stylish and well-groomed. Every morning after breakfast, I dress and apply makeup for the day. Do you see the glass half empty or half full? I have a very positive attitude about most things, and I always have something to smile about. I have bared my soul to you. I hope you have benefited from it.

CHAPTER 28

How Did You Meet Harry, and How Did That Change Your Life?

This is the best part of this book and my life!

During our lifetime, we meet many people. Some we pass by, and others influence us greatly. But never at this point in my life did I expect to meet someone as special as Harry. I would like to share this experience with you.

It was 5:00 p.m. on Saturday, February 16, 2019, and I had just completed a boring day at home doing various chores. I had no plans for that evening, but echoing in my mind were the words, "Why don't you join us at the Living Room?" My girlfriend and her boyfriend go there every Saturday night to dance. The music is great, and it's a fun place to spend an evening. I had not been there recently, so I decided to join them. I do not believe in fate (*bashert*), but there was some force or whatever that influenced that decision.

When I arrived at the Living Room, I saw my friends sitting with another couple. As I approached the table, they greeted me warmly. Harry pulled a chair for me between him and the other woman. I realized immediately that they were not a couple. The guys started to tell jokes that were very funny. I contributed with several jokes of my own. The evening was hilarious! At the end of the evening, Harry left and never asked for my phone number. I thought that he was not interested in me, and anyway, he seemed to be too young. This was my rationalization!

Evidently, he was interested, got my number, and called me the next morning for a date. I was very surprised to hear from him. I still thought he was too young, but what did I have to lose? It was just a date for dinner. Little did I realize that this man was going to be the love of my life!

On our first date, Harry wore white pants, a blue shirt, and navy blazer with a blue hanky in the jacket pocket. I was impressed! How different from the Florida attire of jeans and a polo shirt. We had dinner at the Capitol Grill in Boca. Harry mentioned his age very casually, and I was relieved to find that he was not as young as I had previously thought but closer to my age. During the evening, he told me that he had written numerous books and published five of them. They are on Amazon. I had never met an author. He was also involved with different businesses and loved negotiating deals. He started with a small courier service in Philadelphia, which he developed into a large multistate business, where he employed over five hundred people. His company was recognized by INC magazine three years in a row as one of the fastest-growing privately owned companies. I particularly loved his stories and sense of humor. Once again, I was impressed!

Harry is a devoted father, grandfather, and great-grandfather. He has two daughters. Susan, married to Marc Howard, spends her time between Philadelphia and Boca; and Beth lives in Philadelphia, Pennsylvania. His wife had passed away recently. She had a stroke, and he had been her caretaker for the last thirteen years. After she passed away, he relocated from Philadelphia to Florida and rented at Boca West. He never thought that he would meet someone so soon before he had an opportunity to meet all the single ladies at Boca. They were upset, but how lucky for me! At the same time, I told Harry my entire background from the time I lived in the Bronx to now in Boca. After Harry and I bared our souls and finished a delicious dinner, he drove me home. He bid me goodbye with a peck on the cheek and said, "We'll be in touch."

An interesting anecdote:

The day following our first date, Harry's daughter asked him if he called Mimi. Harry replied, "Why should I call her? She was perfectly OK when I left her." Harry having not dated for almost fifty years, had no idea as to what she was talking about. "You are supposed to call the next day to see if she had a good time, Dad." Harry thought for a minute and said, "What if she tells me that she didn't have a good time?" His daughter laughed and replied, "Then, I guess that's the end of the romance." Well fortunately, it turned out that we had a great time, and it was the start of the most exciting year of my life!

It didn't take long before we found ourselves dating on a regular basis. We went to every event that Boca West offered. We loved to dance and enjoyed being with people. Harry was always the life of the party. He had a "hatful of jokes" that he told with great timing and expression. This made everyone laugh and love him, including my family; my friends Ilene, Dallas, and Mimi L. . . . and especially me!

During our courtship and to this day, he is kind and thoughtful. He loves buying me all kinds of gifts. Sometimes, I am embarrassed because he had just given me something the previous week. I never met anyone who was so generous and only wants to make me happy. And he does make me happy because he is so funny with his jokes and stories. He constantly writes poems and stories about us. I laugh all day, which should help me live to one hundred twenty years!

We spent the year having the best time of our lives. Harry had never been on a cruise, so when my family made plans to go on a cruise, he was invited. We entered a *Dancing with the Stars* contest. He was selected and won! We also went on a cruise to Canada with my brother, Morty, and Helen. For my birthday in September, we went to Monte Carlo. It was wonderful, and Harry was wonderful! For New Year's, we flew to Las Vegas and spent New Year's Eve seeing the Lady Gaga show in the sixth row. It was great!

CHAPTER 29

How Did Your Life Change During the Coronavirus Pandemic?

Suddenly, the entire world changed! It is difficult for me to believe that this coronavirus pandemic was in the process of destroying the lifestyles that we all took for granted. I often think about the last week before we had to quarantine ourselves in order to survive. Sunday, we had dinner with family; Monday, we saw a nice film; Tuesday, I performed in a song review; Wednesday, we went to dinner and a show; Friday, we had dinner with friends. All of these events took place at Boca West. And then, like every place elsewhere, Boca West had closed all of its activities . . . tennis, golf, fitness, spa, restaurants, lectures, shows, the pool, etc. Of course, the difficulties that other people were experiencing brings a little sobriety to our situation.

We were so fortunate to have each other during this terrible time. When we think about what was happening around us, it seemed more like a nightmare rather than reality. Entire countries were shut down, millions of people were infected, hundred thousands of people were dying, and people all over the world were being told to stay in their homes. Senior citizens were the greatest victims. They were more vulnerable because their immune systems have weakened with age. We were in that category, and that made us additionally frightened that we may get it!

We decided that we must abide by social distancing, as it is called, to the extreme! We did not leave our house except for a necessary visit to a doctor. Some visits were done remotely through FaceTime—if you had an iPhone. We sometimes took a car ride, and we always remained in the car. Fortunately, we live in a beautiful house with a back patio overlooking a lake and fountain. Harry spent his day creating funny poems or writing another book. I spent my time trying to keep the house in order, preparing meals, doing laundry, etc. Occasionally, Harry would cook something for lunch or dinner. There was always a project that I was working on, such as knitting baby sweaters, crocheting evening bags, making throw pillows, etc. I sometimes watched the series that were made in Turkey in the afternoon, and then we watched a movie at night.

We had all our meals together. We were always thinking about what we were going to eat for lunch or dinner and what we had to order from Instacart. We dealt primarily with Publix and Amazon. We did not go to any store but had everything delivered. We felt safer that way. After dinner, we played backgammon, Rummikub, scrabble, or gin rummy. As you can see, we were very busy and seldom bored. Harry always said something to make me laugh, and I smiled all the time.

We also spent a great deal of time on the iPhone. Thank goodness for FaceTime! I had not seen most of my family in a long time. They were all working virtually in their respective homes. Those in school were home or in college but learning remotely. Harry was in touch with his family as well. We had planned on going to New York at this time but had to cancel everything. We could not wait until this terrible virus was over. We are now trying to resume our life as it was before the pandemic.

The following is one of Harry's poems.

When Mimi was writing this chapter, I was always there for her; that made us both feel good.
But when we talked about the people affected by the virus, it was
difficult to imagine how they felt; no one could.
It is very strange to have such mixed feelings at this same time.
I guess it's a human emotion too difficult to define.
On the one hand, we both felt safe and happy living in our gated community home
And then on the other hand sad because of all the people affected
by the virus who were sick and alone.
When we looked back and thought about all the good times we had
last year,
We never could have imagined the entire world would now be living in such fear.
I am so grateful to have Mimi to share my life.
It helps me get through this time of turmoil and strife.
I said to Mimi, "Let's not count the days as they mount,
But rather let us make each day count."
So we hope and pray that by the time you are reading this book,
the coronavirus is in our past.
So then we can get back to our lives as we knew them at last.

CHAPTER 30

Tell Me about Being in Love in Your Twilight Years.

This may be the last chapter of this book, but it certainly is not the last chapter of my life. Harry and I wake up each day, anxious to spend the day together. We sometimes reminisce about the past, but more importantly, we are so lucky to have each other. It's hard to believe that you can meet someone in your twilight years and have a love affair that is beyond something you have ever experienced and that you are living the best time of your life.

Looking back, I wonder what my life would be like if on that particular night, I had not gone to the Living Room. Was it fate, or was it destiny? Whatever it was, I cannot imagine my life without Harry! Sometimes, we sit on our patio overlooking the lake to watch the sun set. There are no secrets between us. We have opened our hearts to one another and have the same dreams and desires. We are in love and are enjoying life to the fullest.

There is an expression, "It's a shame that youth is wasted on the young." Harry and I are competing with that expression. We are engaging in all activities and enjoying every event that we participate in. Now you know I am that little girl who lived in the Bronx and is now living the American dream at Boca West Country Club. We have a positive attitude and know that tomorrow will be better, and the day after that will even be better!

The best is yet to come.

"I Want to Tell You about Mimi"

(A poem from Harry)

She is a warm, caring woman like no other

Her only sibling was one brother

She grew up having to make her own way

Now look what she has become today

She was a wife, a mother, and a grandparent too

And a teacher, a sculptress, and a seamstress that made old things look like new

She loves to dance, still plays tennis and cooks up a storm

Those lucky enough to know her will agree that besides all of this, she is tender and warm

So I have told you a little about Mimi, but now that you have
read this book, you have learned all the rest

What more can I say . . . she is the very best

Harry 12/1/22

Me And Harry

My Family

MIMI SHERMAN

Printed in the United States
by Baker & Taylor Publisher Services